Random Thoughts of Healing

Janette Mercado Gonzalvo
Author

About the Author

Janette Gonzalvo adores stories and dreams of being a reporter to be able to share news and knowledge with others, while aspiring to be a writer. Since she was young, she has kept a journal where she pours out her feelings, especially when she feels sad or angry. In high school and college, she was always involved in the school newspaper because she enjoyed writing articles that could help her peers.

She is passionate about spreading awareness and kindness through various means, including public speaking. She joined the International Toastmasters Club to improve her speaking skills and further her journey as a writer.

She believes that everyone has a unique story to tell and hopes that her stories will inspire others to embrace their individuality and pursue their dreams, eventually turning them into reality.

This book is for everyone who's finding it hard to move forward and heal. It's meant to help you understand that what you're going through is something many others experience too, and you're not alone. Whether you're dealing with a heartbreak or loss, or just trying to find your way after a tough time, this book is like a friendly hand to guide you through.

Table of Contents

Chapter 1: Random Thoughts of Healing An Overview 1

Chapter 2: Random Thoughts of Healing The Heartbreak Experiences 10

Chapter 3: "30 Days of Healing Journey: Lessons Learned" 28

Chapter 4 Healing Stages 72

Chapter 5: Random Thoughts of Healing - Inspirational and Motivational Quotes 96

Chapter 1:
Random Thoughts of Healing
An Overview

Random Thoughts of Healing

The healing thoughts shared in this book stem from my own past relationships and similar experiences my close friends endured after painful breakups. Every idea and thought is derived from tacit and explicit collective knowledge gathered from various resources.

Some might consider breakups a failed relationship, but to me, they're not failures; they are "worthy experiences", "life lessons" and even "blessings". Breaking up can be tough, but sometimes it's for the best. You get the freedom to focus on yourself and what makes you happy without having to consider someone else's feelings all the time. Breakups can teach you a lot about yourself and what you want in a relationship. You learn from the experience and grow as a person. Ending a relationship opens up the possibility of meeting new people and exploring new relationships that might be better for you. If a relationship isn't working out, no matter how hard you're trying, breaking up can bring relief and peace of mind. Knowing that you're no longer in a situation that was causing you stress or unhappiness can bring a sense of relief and freedom.. You can use the time after a breakup to focus on your own hobbies, interests, and goals without having to worry about anyone. Going through a breakup can be tough, but it helps you build resilience and learn how to cope with difficult situations in the future. Breaking up can actually be a good thing. Just think, without experiencing heartbreak, how would you discover enlightenment, learn about boundaries, set standards for yourself, or even understand the importance of self-love and self-care?

Going through tough times in relationships, even traumatic or toxic ones, can teach you how to treat yourself better and love yourself more deeply. It also helps you understand people's behavior better, much like being a psychologist without a degree. I once saw a post on Instagram about a girl who broke up with her boyfriend and, after three months, she started her own business, hit the gym, and looked amazing. It goes to show that breakups can lead to positive changes.

Some people think of heartbreak as purely negative, but in reality, it can lead to positive growth after dealing with the pain of breaking up. It's kind of ironic, isn't it? Remember, even though breakups can be hard, they can also lead to positive changes and growth in the long run.

Establishing boundaries and standards is crucial for both men and women, as it not only boosts our self-esteem but also promotes healthy relationships. . These boundaries are aimed at safeguarding our mental health and overall well-being by helping us prioritize our time and energy. However, achieving these goals often requires enduring painful experiences, such as feeling lost, experiencing self-pity, and facing various emotional challenges. While there's a common belief that time can heal all wounds, I personally subscribe to the idea that healing comes from acceptance rather than expectation.

Random Thoughts of Healing

Two key concepts that aid in the process of moving on are the "Law of Detachment" and the "Let Them Go Theory". These principles will be further explained in the subsequent chapter of this book. Regardless of how much time has passed by, if one remains fixated on hope without acknowledging and accepting reality, true progress cannot be made. However, embracing the notion that "it is what it is" enables us to swiftly move forward in life, recognizing our worth and believing that we deserve the best that the world has to offer.

Think of life as a book where each experience turns a new page, propelling us into the next chapter. Rather than dwelling on the past, it's essential to view past experiences as valuable lessons and reminders of our inherent worth as human beings. All of us are deserving of love, care, and attention, and understanding this makes us realize that we are the prize in our own lives.

The Law of Detachment in a healing journey is like letting go of a helium balloon. Imagine holding onto that balloon tightly—it can't float away. But when you release your grip, it rises effortlessly. Similarly, in healing, detachment means releasing our grip on outcomes and expectations. It's about accepting that we can't control everything, especially in matters of healing. We might want a specific result—a quick recovery, for instance—but clinging to that desire too tightly can create unnecessary stress. Instead, by detaching, we open ourselves to the flow of healing energy, allowing it to work its magic in its own time and way. Detachment doesn't mean giving up or being indifferent; rather, it's a mindset of trust and surrender, believing that whatever happens is ultimately for our highest good.

Moreover, the Law of Detachment invites us to let go of past hurts and grievances that may be blocking our healing journey. Just as clutter fills a room, holding onto old resentments fills our hearts and minds, leaving little space for healing to occur. Detachment frees us from the chains of bitterness and resentment, allowing us to move forward with clarity and openness. It's like cleaning out a closet—you make space for new, positive energy to flow in. By releasing the past and staying present in the moment, we create a fertile ground for healing to take root and flourish. In essence, the Law of Detachment teaches us to trust the process, release control, and embrace the journey with an open heart and mind.

The "Let them go" theory is a powerful concept in the journey of healing, urging individuals to release the burdens of their past and embrace the present moment. This theory suggests that holding onto past grievances, regrets, or negative emotions only serves to weigh us down, hindering our ability to move forward and experience true healing. By letting go, we free ourselves from the chains of resentment and bitterness, allowing space for growth, acceptance, and inner peace. It's like unclenching a tightly closed fist to open our hands to receive the gifts of life anew.

Random Thoughts of Healing

In practical terms, letting go involves acknowledging our feelings without letting them consume us, forgiving ourselves and others for past mistakes, and making a conscious choice to focus on what we can control in the present rather than dwelling on what has already happened. It's about recognizing that while we cannot change the past, we have the power to shape our future by releasing the grip of past pain. Letting go doesn't mean forgetting or condoning hurtful actions; rather, it's a radical act of self-love and empowerment, allowing us to reclaim our inner peace and move forward with renewed clarity and strength. As we embark on our healing journey, embracing the "let them go" theory can be a transformative step towards liberation and emotional well-being.

Each person has their own unique ways of dealing with their emotions and finding ways to feel better, valued, and loved. Recovering from pain isn't a quick process—it can take weeks, months, or even years for some. Some people seek a rebound relationship to move on, while others try to keep busy to distract themselves. Some may make unhealthy choices, while others focus on improving themselves in their careers and lives. Some become cynical about love and develop anxiety.

Understanding basic human psychology helps us see that our actions and those of our ex-partners are sometimes influenced by unresolved childhood traumas. It's crucial to address these traumas to cultivate happy and fulfilling relationships in the future. Many of you may already recognize feelings of abandonment and anxiety, which we'll explore further in the latter part of this book for deeper understanding.

When we talk about abandonment style in a healing journey, we're delving into how someone copes with feelings of being left behind or neglected. It's like an emotional fingerprint that shapes how we see relationships and handle separations. For some, abandonment might mean feeling anxious or scared when someone they care about isn't around. Others might become fiercely independent, pushing people away before they can leave first. Understanding your abandonment style is like finding a map when lost– it shows where you've been and where you might need to go. Healing starts with awareness, recognizing how this style has influenced your life. It's about making peace with the past, forgiving those who left, and learning to trust again, both yourself and others. Building healthy connections becomes the cornerstone of the journey, knowing that even if someone steps away, it doesn't mean you're unworthy or unlovable. It's about rewriting the narrative, turning abandonment from a wound into a scar, a reminder of resilience and growth.

As you navigate through your healing journey, embracing your abandonment style means learning to rewrite your story. It's about acknowledging the pain of abandonment while also recognizing your strength in surviving it. Instead of letting past experiences dictate your present and future, you reclaim your power by reshaping your beliefs about love, trust, and connection. This journey isn't about erasing the past but rather reframing it, seeing it through a lens of compassion and understanding. It's like tending to a garden – pulling out the weeds of doubt and fear, and nurturing the seeds of self-worth and acceptance. Surrounding yourself with supportive relationships becomes crucial, finding those who will hold space for your healing without judgment. Ultimately, the healing journey transforms abandonment from a source of fear into a catalyst for growth, paving the way for deeper connections and a more fulfilling life.

Healing from an anxious attachment style can be a journey filled with self-discovery and growth. Anxious attachment often stems from a fear of abandonment or rejection, leading individuals to crave constant reassurance and closeness in relationships. Throughout this journey, it's crucial to first recognize and acknowledge these feelings without judgment. Understanding the root causes of anxious attachment can help individuals develop self-compassion and empathy for themselves.

As part of the healing process, learning to set boundaries is essential. This means recognizing one's own needs and communicating them effectively in relationships. It involves finding a balance between seeking connection and maintaining independence. Developing a secure sense of self can also be a key aspect of healing from anxious attachment. This might involve exploring personal interests, values, and goals outside of romantic relationships. Building a support network of friends, family, or a therapist can provide additional guidance and encouragement along the way. Ultimately, healing from anxious attachment involves patience, self-reflection, and a willingness to cultivate healthier patterns of relating to others.

In the upcoming chapters, I'll share some thoughts that may challenge you but are worth considering. I'll delve into different stages of healing and share insights from my own experiences with heartbreak.

Chapter 2:
Random Thoughts of Healing
The Heartbreak Experiences

The heartbreak experiences I've faced in my own life have shaped who I am today. From the pain of a breakup to the disappointment of unfulfilled expectations, each one has taught me valuable lessons about love, resilience, and self-discovery.

One particularly memorable heartbreak was when I thought I had found "the one", only to have the relationship end abruptly. I felt lost and confused, wondering what I had done wrong and if I would ever find love again. But as time passed, I realized that this heartbreak was a blessing in disguise. It forced me to reevaluate what I truly wanted in a partner and in life, and it ultimately led me to a deeper understanding of myself.

Another heartbreak came in the form of a friendship that fell apart. Losing someone I trusted and cared about deeply was incredibly painful, and it took time to come to terms with the loss. But through this experience, I learned the importance of setting boundaries and surrounding myself with people who uplift and support me.

While heartbreak is never easy to endure, I've come to see it as an opportunity for growth and self-reflection. Each experience, no matter how painful, has helped me become stronger, more resilient, and more compassionate toward myself and others. And though the scars may remain, they serve as a reminder of the love I've experienced and the lessons I've learned along the way.

Random Thoughts of Healing

I used to not like talking about my personal life with people I don't know, but now I'm writing a book. My goal is to inspire people who have been through heartbreak and want to move forward. I'm sharing my stories because I hope others can learn from what I've been through. I want to explain how I got to where I am today. Even though I'm not in a relationship, I feel complete on my own. In the past, my relationships brought me a lot of pain. I felt insecure, lost my confidence, and went through deep emotional struggles. I felt mentally exhausted and started to doubt everything. I had issues with feeling abandoned, anxious, and trusting others. But now, I'm focused on my life. I have a purpose and I'm an inspiration to many. We all have unique abilities, and sometimes going through tough times helps us discover our strengths. It motivates us to chase our dreams. For example, I never thought I could be a writer. But writing became a way for me to express my emotions and heal. If someone hurts you, writing can help. It's a powerful way to heal and express yourself. I've written articles at work about hard work paying off, "The Pathway to Success", "How everyone is valuable" and "Aspire to Achieve". My colleagues loved them because they were based on real experiences. Their positive feedback inspired me to keep writing. Now, I always carry a journal with me to jot down random thoughts, anywhere and anytime. Producing my own book is one of my biggest goals. Writing has become my passion, and I'm grateful for how it has touched others.

Reading self-help books became a big part of my life too. They played a crucial role in helping me deal with my traumas and understanding that everything happens for a reason. These books have taught me a great deal about people's emotions and feelings, which made me stop judging them based on their actions alone. I realized that everyone has their own struggles, and it's important to empathize rather than judge. Self-help books offer valuable insights and strategies to get unstuck from tough situations. I started building a collection of these books and enjoyed sharing the wisdom I gained from them. I believe in the power of knowledge gained through both personal experiences and reading. Having these two references lends credibility to your words. That's why they say, "Knowledge is power," and life experiences are the best teachers. You truly understand the value of self healing books when you've gone through deep pain yourself.

Also, I started public speaking after I joined the International Toastmaster club. There, I met different types of people and learned from them. My confidence grew, and I got better at talking in front of others. I used to be scared of being on stage, but I overcame that fear. I wrote my own speeches and shared them with many audiences. I even got asked to organize events, become the Chief Sergeant at Arms, and write articles for their magazine. In the end, going through a breakup turned out to be a good thing because it helped me discover more about myself outside of my comfort zone.

Random Thoughts of Healing

Keep moving forward and releasing the past. There are amazing things waiting for you in life. Even when times are hard, believe that better days are coming. It's okay to face challenges, but keep striving to get better. Don't think of yourself as a victim; focus on the good things. Don't doubt your worth just because someone left you. You are valuable, and the right person will recognize that, even without you doing anything extraordinary to impress them.

Let me share my heartbreak stories

I was 20 years old when I experienced my first heartbreak. I won't go into too much detail, but my time with him seemed like a movie. We were together for about two years, and the first year was filled with fun, sweetness, and romance. However, as we both got busier with our jobs, we started seeing each other less due to conflicting schedules. Then one day, I had a strange feeling, a "gut feeling" that something wasn't right. When making a major decision, always listen to your gut because it can warn you of potential dangers.

My cousin unexpectedly visited me and showed me a picture of my ex with another girl at the mall, holding hands while he was still with me. The mall was close by, so I rushed there and saw them myself. I didn't think clearly; I confronted them in front of everyone, shaking and crying. I wanted to confront the girl physically, but my ex stopped me. He just kept her away from me. We talked, and I grabbed his phone, finding their messages where he said, "I love you, my Tin." I was shocked; my ex had been talking about this girl to me nonstop, complaining about her being talkative and loud, which he found very annoying. Then, I realized that if your partner keeps complaining about someone in detail, it might mean they're interested in that person and, in my case, it turned out to be true.

He asked for a breakup, even begged for it. But I was foolish; I didn't accept it. Instead, I told him he could be with that girl as long as he stayed with me. Essentially, I gave him permission to cheat if he didn't leave me. I couldn't imagine life without him and convinced myself he was just confused or infatuated with the other girl. I was in denial and couldn't believe he had fallen in love with someone else. He listened quietly, then begged me to go home, promising we'd talk about the relationship again once we both had clear minds. But he only said that to calm me down and get me to leave. Looking back, it's embarrassing and I laugh at myself now. You'll laugh at your past embarrassing moments once you've completely moved on from your ex, questioning why you did certain things.

Since I didn't accept the breakup, I acted like everything was fine. I kept texting, calling, and visiting him, becoming overly clingy and toxic. The more I chased him, the more he distanced himself. But I couldn't stop. I became a stalker, a paranoid, and a withdrawn person. I cried because I couldn't accept that he left me for someone else. I doubted and blamed myself, thinking I should have been a better girlfriend. I was depressed, obsessed, and neglected my work until I got fired. I had no life and felt like a loser. My father was upset because I refused to talk to anyone, eat, or work – all I wanted was my ex. I became even more toxic, begging him to leave the girl and choose me instead. I kept seeing him, checking his phone, and feeling sorry for myself when I saw their happy pictures and videos together.

I was completely drained, exhausted in every way – emotionally, mentally, and physically. I had no other option but to surrender and draw closer to God. So, I did. I started visiting churches every Wednesday and Sunday, praying for my ex to come back and love me like he used to. But then, something unexpected happened. I saw my ex and his new girlfriend together in the same church on the same day. I couldn't understand why. Was it a punishment? I was confused. Later, I realized that maybe the universe wanted me to see them together to understand the kind of person he was and what my future would look like if I stayed with him. It was like history repeating itself – my ex had left this same girl before and found someone new. It was a painful realization, and I started doubting myself, feeling insecure compared to her. I lost my self-confidence, became less cheerful, and overthought everything. These were the scars from staying in a situation of pity.

But then, I decided it was enough. I let them go, despite the pain, it took a while or even years then finally found peace. I began working on myself, found a new job as an English instructor at a college in the Philippines, and even pursued a Master's degree. It paid off – my salary increased because of the additional qualification. I learned that when you choose to let go, new opportunities emerge, and new doors open for you.

I met my second ex-partner.

A narcissistic energy sucker and expert manipulator. I was with my second ex-partner, who was really good at manipulating and draining my energy. Being in a relationship with him hurt me a lot mentally. I think maybe because of my bad experiences, I settled for less than what I really deserved. In my first breakup, I blamed myself for not trying hard enough, so in my second relationship, I tried to do everything to make it work. I was the one taking charge, buying him expensive gifts, giving him money, and even letting him live in my house. I was always the one making the effort to keep the relationship going, while he just stayed at home, doing drugs and gambling. He would accuse me of things like cheating on him, even though I was trying my hardest to keep him happy, giving him everything I had. I tolerated his behavior because I was scared of being alone. Because of this, I wasted ten years of my life with him, thinking I would never find love again. I let him treat me badly, believing his lies that no one else would ever care about me like he did. Well, I can say that there is no time wasted because I believed that it was meant to happen and brought me a lot of enlightenment about life.

He didn't put any effort into our relationship. I can't remember a single time when he bought me gifts or flowers. He didn't understand when I was going through mood swings

Random Thoughts of Healing

during my period; he just dismissed it as drama. Every time we argued, he'd threaten to leave, pack his things, and I'd end up begging him to stay and apologizing, even though I didn't start the fight. I was just scared of being alone, so I kept giving him chances. Even with three jobs, I was still struggling financially, so I decided to look for work abroad. We ended up in a long-distance relationship, which made my anxiety worse. I would call him repeatedly if he didn't answer, and even check with our neighbors when he didn't respond. Sometimes he'd ignore me for days or weeks, only getting in touch when he needed money. He'd act sweet and give me attention, which led me to keep sending him money until I was deeply in debt. I didn't buy myself anything nice or take care of myself because all my focus was on him, not even on my family or myself.

Until one day, my sister told me that my ex was already addicted to drugs and buried in debt. He'd even turned my home into a drug den for him and his friends. I returned home to try and fix things, but eventually, I had to kick him out. His family begged me to forgive him and give him another chance. I fell victim to his manipulation once again, hoping he'd change. But each chance I gave him took a toll on my mental health. I became toxic, angry, and closed-minded, and there were times when I even considered ending my own life because I couldn't bear the toxicity anymore.

Then, one day, I reached a breaking point and mustered the courage to end our ten-year relationship. It was the best decision I ever made. I felt like I had escaped from a prison. I finally had freedom to breathe without the weight of mental abuse. I began focusing on myself, buying new clothes, bags, shoes, and accessories. I started taking care of myself, getting makeovers, doing my hair, lashes, and nails. I transformed into a new version of myself, feeling younger and happier than I had in years. The joyful, positive, and attractive person I used to be was back, and that's who I am now.

God truly works in mysterious ways. He sees our burdens, our suffering, and hears even the things we haven't spoken aloud. That's why He finds a way to help us out of difficult situations and get away from harmful people. I'm living proof of this truth. Even after leaving my ex, I allowed him to stay and helped him out of kindness and compassion, not love. I knew he had nowhere else to go and no job to support himself. Then, I heard the news that he was arrested for drug possession, while on the same day, I received the biggest promotion of my career from the company I worked for. It felt like an abundance of blessings poured in once I removed him from my life. God's grace is incredible. When we have faith and surrender everything to him, life becomes better. Remember, when you remove negative influences or toxic people from your life, new doors, opportunities, and blessings appear. You'll attract the right people into your life. Trust in God's plan, and things will fall into place.

Random Thoughts of Healing

How do I view my third heartbreak as simply a lesson?

Do you think it's true when people say, "the right love at the wrong time"? Everyone has their own thoughts about it, but I don't believe it. If two people truly love each other and are ready to fight for their love no matter what, there's no such thing as bad timing. That's how I met the third man in my life. I won't go into details, but my life was really complicated when we met. I actually knew him from before because I interviewed him for a job and we hired him because he had great qualifications, good communication skills, and a nice personality. I was the one who had to call the people we hired to tell them they got the job. So, he had my contact info and would message me on WhatsApp if he had questions about the job. Sometimes, I was a bit rude in my responses, not because I'm naturally rude, but because I was super busy arranging my business visa for a three-month training in India. On my first day of training in India, he also had his first day of training in the UAE. My boss asked me to handle the training program for new employees, including him. We had sessions every day for a month, and I was the first person they'd ask if they had questions about the products or processes. We communicated through MS Teams because I was in India for almost seven months, and we all had to work from home because of COVID.

When I met him, he was already engaged, and I was still in a relationship with my second ex-partner. Then, after two years of working from home, the management decided to change the work setup, scheduling it by batches and rotations.

By some twist of fate, we ended up on the same schedule. Anyway, this guy didn't really like me because I was often rude and unapproachable towards him. I would always turn down his requests until he decided he would never ask me for anything again, even if I were the only person left on Earth. I didn't realize how much he disliked me until we started talking, and he confessed it to me. On the first day we returned to the office after two years, something changed. For some reason, he caught my attention, and I became really interested in him. There was a sudden spark and happiness in my heart that I hadn't felt in the past 10 years.

    I believed and knew that the feeling was mutual the first time we locked eyes. He had lost a lot of weight, and his eyes looked very sad. I could sense his pain, though I didn't understand why. On his first day, he had a problem with his headset but didn't come to me about it. Instead, he went to another supervisor on the floor. That supervisor told him he needed to talk to me since I handled those things. So, he had no choice but to come to me if he wanted to take calls. I helped him sort out his headset, and I was really happy in that moment. I kept smiling and stealing glances at him, and I noticed he was looking at me too. Every day at work, I make it a point to say hi to all my colleagues before starting. I went over to his desk and said to him, "Hello! With a blush smile?" He looked so different after losing weight. He explained that his significant weight loss was a result of intense exercise routines and some personal struggles. Then I asked him, "Why do you seem sad?"

because I could see the sadness in his eyes and somehow, I could feel it too.

It sounds like we had our first real conversation, and he opened up to me about his broken engagement due to family conflicts. He was going through a lot of pain and anger because of it. At the same time, I was dealing with a toxic relationship with my ex-partner. As we talked more each day, we got comfortable sharing our personal lives, our heartaches, engaging in deep conversations. I'll never forget when he told me I seemed like I was just going through the motions of life without really living it. I was neglecting myself, just working endlessly to support my whole family, including my ex. I shared openly about how my ex was using me and my money, with me doing all the providing and him just taking advantage. He got annoyed hearing about my excuses, but I still defended my ex. We shared our stories, our pain, our sadness, our joys, and our dreams. With each passing day, I found myself liking him more and more. I couldn't wait to see him and talk to him again. Eventually, I decided to dress nicely and put on makeup because I wanted to look good for him. When he complimented me, saying "nice outfit" and "You look pretty," those simple words meant a lot to me because I hadn't heard such compliments from my ex.

We began exchanging messages after work, talking for hours, and eventually started seeing each other in person too. But before I started seeing him, I ended things with my ex. Some people might judge me for moving on so quickly, but believe me when I say that leaving my ex was the best and happiest decision I ever made. He taught me how to love and care for myself. He helped me see my own value and worth. We became each other's support, both of us needing someone to talk to during our broken times. In short, we were each other's rebound, but in a positive way. I still remember our first date, which lasted for only 15 minutes. It was the same day I decided to leave my ex, not because I found someone new, but because I was completely done with the relationship. He was simply the catalyst for me to realize the truth, to wake up from my foolishness, and to stop wasting my time with my ex. My family, relatives, friends, and colleagues were all happy to hear that my previous ex and I were finally over. I have no regrets about leaving him, even now.

This new guy and I made things official, and he introduced me to his family and closest friends. We started spending more time together, and he treated me well. He made me happy, made me feel special, and it was the first time I truly felt loved. I engaged in conversations about gender equality with him, and everything was good in the first six months of our relationship. We became each other's support system, always there for each other through ups and downs. I was there for his struggles and successes, and he was always by my side, offering advice and being a great listener. He was the guy I had prayed for, and he completely transformed my life. I became a better version of myself—I started going to the salon, wearing makeup, dressing up, and taking better care of my body. I learned to prioritize myself because of him, and he became my hero.

But there were moments when I sensed he wasn't fully over his ex-fiancée. I caught him checking her social media, which broke my heart. When I confronted him, he admitted to still being broken over what happened between them. I also found out he was talking to other girls at his new job, which hurt me deeply. My anxiety, trauma, and insecurities resurfaced, and I felt paranoid. I investigated and discovered he was still talking to his ex-fiancée. Again, he didn't deny it and apologized, acknowledging that I deserved better. Despite this, we continued our relationship, even though he believed we could never have a future together due to our age difference, my life complications, and our conflicting beliefs. He felt his society wouldn't accept my complicated life, and instead of resenting it, he thought it best for us to separate and move on.

I became clingy, constantly calling and messaging him, out of fear. He changed how he treated me, and our relationship became toxic. Eventually, I decided to set him free and break up with him because I didn't want to feel paranoid anymore, I didn't want a relationship that felt forced, and I wanted to be chosen despite my circumstances. I thought he was my happy ending, but he turned out to be another lesson in my life. I started questioning myself again, wondering why I wasn't enough, why he couldn't choose me.

Even though we're not together anymore, we still keep in touch. He treats me kindly, making me feel special, by occasionally buying me gifts and bringing me to his friends and family at events or parties. We've been like this for almost 2 years and 6 months. But I started becoming toxic and obsessed again. I couldn't stop checking his social media and questioning him about other girls, even though we weren't committed.

Our relationship was more of a situationship, where I didn't have any rights. Still, he always tried to spend time with me, calling and checking up on me. Some days went smoothly, while others were marked by conflict. I accused him of cheating, even though I didn't have the right to be jealous or stop him from talking to others. I know I acted immaturely, but my actions are merely a reflection of his actions towards me and an indication that I am still struggling with previous trauma that that needs to be addressed. He never gives me false hope and he's honest about our arrangement from the start.

Things reached a breaking point when he didn't treat me special on Valentine's Day. I expected flowers or gifts, but got nothing. I confronted him about it and asked him, "Am I not worthy of flowers or gifts?" When I asked him about it, he said we weren't in a relationship, and therefore, he didn't have to give me anything. That hurt me deeply. I started to move on and distance myself from him. He stopped calling for days, then weeks. When he finally did contact me, we fought again, and I kept asking if he had found someone new. I just wanted him to be honest so I could stop hoping for a chance with him. He got angry and decided to end our situationship and just be friends. I'm thinking too much that maybe the reason he only wants to be friends is because he's found someone else.

I accepted it because I remembered from my first heartbreak that I should never beg for love and attention. I didn't want to live in one-sided love anymore. I regained my self-respect and value, knowing that I deserved better.. I am not denying that it was somehow painful for me, but I mainly focused on myself, striving hard to achieve my goals. I found opportunities like hosting events and becoming a communication and soft skills trainer. I even wrote my own book, got invited by some groups to write an article for the top International Toastmasters Newsletter, and made an Instagram page called @randomthoughts_healing to support others going through what I'd been through.

In my next chapter, I'll share how I managed to heal and become a better version of myself. Overall, my ex wasn't a bad person. He taught me a lot and supported me in my successes, which is why he'll always have a special place in my heart. We've decided to be friends, and I'm at peace with that. I'm happy now because I feel whole again. I no longer rely on someone else for my happiness. As I've mentioned before, there are numerous paths to finding happiness, and that's what I'm actively pursuing now.

The lesson I've got from this heartbreak is never involve yourself in a 'situationship' as it's simply a waste of time, delaying the right person for you. A situationship is when two people are spending time together and maybe even have feelings for each other, but they haven't really decided if they're in a serious relationship or not. It's like being in a gray area between friendship and romance, where things are somewhat undefined and uncertain. A male friend once told me, men can usually figure out if a woman is right for them within six months. This means they can determine whether they want to be with her long-term after spending half a year together. During these months, they pay attention to how they feel when they're together, how they communicate, and if they share similar values and goals. It's like a trial period to see if the relationship has a strong foundation for the future.

Some relationships come into our lives because they're meant to, while others are like lessons from God or opportunities for personal growth. Sometimes, people enter our lives to teach us important lessons or to inspire us to become better versions of ourselves. They might challenge us, support us, or help us discover our strengths and weaknesses. These relationships can be valuable in shaping who we are and guiding us toward our true selves.

If you're reading this message, I want you to know how grateful I am that you've been a part of my life. I deeply appreciate the moments we've shared, and I'll always hold onto those memories close to my heart. You've brought joy, laughter, and warmth into my life, and I cherish every single one of those precious moments we've experienced together.

Chapter 3:
"30 Days of Healing Journey: Lessons Learned"

For a whole month, I wrote down how I was feeling every day as I tried to get better. I did this because I wanted to help others understand how I managed to deal with healing. I'll talk about the things I did that helped me, the stuff I did every day, and why it helped me. Even though I haven't fully recovered yet, I'm feeling much, much better now. I don't feel hurt, angry, or sad like I used to. Instead, I feel genuinely happy and like I'm whole again. It's important to remember that everyone's path to healing is different, so you don't have to do exactly what I did. But I hope my journal can give you some ideas to start your own journey toward feeling better.

The journey of healing is like walking along a path, where consistency, patience, and determination act as guiding stars in the night sky. Each step forward may seem small, but it's the steady pace that brings progress. Consistency means showing up, even on the tough days, and putting in the effort, whether it's taking care of your body, mind, or soul. Patience is the gentle reminder that healing doesn't happen overnight; it's a gradual process, like the slow unfolding of a flower bud. And determination is the fuel that keeps you going, even when obstacles arise. It's the belief that you can and will overcome whatever challenges come your way. So, as you walk this path, remember not to worry, for everything will eventually fall into place. Trust in the journey, trust in yourself, and know that at the end of it all, there's light waiting to greet you.

Random Thoughts of Healing

Day 1:

I have decided to temporarily deactivate all my social media accounts. This step is essential for me to avoid the temptation of checking his social media or viewing his stories, as these actions tend to trigger my emotions. By doing so, I can redirect my focus towards myself, particularly towards achieving my goals without any distractions.

I made up my mind after going through really tough times. I saw that I hadn't been treating myself well, and I didn't want to feel hurt anymore. Even though I was feeling upset inside, I didn't say anything because I was scared that if I did, he might leave me completely. When I let him back in without any limits, I felt really uneasy. The voice inside me scolded me, asking why I let him treat me poorly when I should have stood up for myself. That night, I slept poorly, feeling unhappy and unsatisfied.

This realization served as a wake-up call—I deserved better. It became evident that I needed to let go of someone who didn't see my importance and made me settle for mere crumbs of affection. I made a promise to myself never to disrespect my own worth for the sake of anyone. I resolved that losing him would be preferable to losing myself again.

After everything that happened, I found comfort in making a list of reasons why he wasn't the right person for me. I wondered if staying in that relationship was making me feel more bad than good. Was it making me feel peaceful and safe? Thinking about these questions helped me decide that it was time to let go and move forward.

On my first day without social media, I succeeded in keeping him off my mind and refrained from mentioning his name. Despite the difficulty, I persevered, recognizing the need for self-control. I took further steps by deleting his contacts, with plans to block his number soon. I was steadfastly committed to this course of action, fully aware that it was essential for my own well-being.. I learned the importance of self-value and self-respect, and I refused to let anyone undermine them.

It's perfectly fine to say goodbye to people who don't deserve to be in our lives. We shouldn't think that good things are rare and we have to hold on to whatever we can get. Instead, we should bravely let go, knowing that we deserve better. Our value as individuals is something we shouldn't compromise on.

Day 2:

It's been really tough, but I know I have to be strong and stick to my decision for my own happiness. This is crucial for my healing and for keeping my eyes on my goals. I've discovered that keeping a journal is incredibly useful. It gives me a way to let out the feelings I'm dealing with, without completely cutting off contact. Besides taking a break from social media, not contacting him at all is also helping me. It gives me the space I need to be myself without thinking about him.

Right now, I'm feeling really sad. I keep wondering why he lost interest in me and could not be happy with my love and care. I've done everything I can to make him pick me over anyone else, but I've realized that no matter how hard I try, if I'm not the one he wants, he'll never choose me. It's really hard to accept this truth, but I know I have to keep going. I need to focus on loving myself and think about the idea that maybe we're just not meant to be together.

Even though I still feel tempted to think about him, I try to shift my focus to other things. I watch TV shows, write in my journal, read self-help books, study, and concentrate on my job to keep my mind off him. They say, "Fake it till you make it," so I'm trying to act like I'm okay until I really am. Taking a break from social media is helping too, and I'll go back to it when I'm feeling better and have completely healed.

Sticking to this choice is really important because I've seen it make a difference in my life. Every day brings its own struggles, but I believe in the idea that you have to go through tough times to get to the good stuff. I won't let myself be exposed to things that might bring up bad feelings, like watching videos about heartbreak or feeling like I'm not good enough. I know my value and I need to stand up for it, not to show anyone else, but to prove it to myself.

The way others treat me comes from how I treat myself. It's all about what's inside me. If I want others to treat me well, I have to treat myself well first. Any disrespect I face is partly because I've allowed it. I don't want to feel bad about myself anymore; I won't let myself wallow in self-pity because I know I deserve more.

Thank you so much, J! Your words mean a lot to me. I've been through a lot, but I'm trying to use those experiences to become stronger and braver. They've taught me so much, and I don't want to forget those lessons. I'll let them be like armor as I heal and keep moving forward. Life keeps going, and I'm going along with it, step by step.

I believe that someday, the right person will come into my life and treat me with the respect and love I deserve. Making it through day 2 shows my strength. Deleting all my social media was a big step for me, showing that I'm taking control of my own happiness. It's the start of a new chapter, and I'm determined to keep moving forward. I know there are better days waiting for me ahead.

Day 3:

I'm still here, standing strong and proud of how I've been sticking to my path. Social media apps are still off my phone, and I'm resisting the urge to check his status on WhatsApp. Thoughts of him come and go, but I'm steadily moving forward. The other day, my cousin mentioned him in conversation, but I smoothly changed the subject. Instead of dwelling on him, I focus on things that matter more to me. It hurts to know he's paying attention to someone else, but I have to accept that change is the only temporary thing in the world. While I know I need to heal on my own, I'm also open to the possibility of cautiously exploring new relationships and connections. Two guys have asked me out, and since I don't have any other plans this weekend, I've decided to go on those dates.

Even with all this, I'm still careful. I make sure that whoever I spend time with respects me and isn't just looking for something easy. I'm not ready to invest my emotions too quickly. Maybe by going through this, I'll finally be able to move forward and give myself a chance. It doesn't hurt to try, right?

If my ex tries to get in touch, I'm determined to ignore his messages and not answer his calls for a while as I focus on what matters. A friend suggested that being angry might help me heal faster, but I'm mostly disappointed in myself for how I've been acting. I feel bad about how I've been in the past—doing things like invading his privacy and begging for his attention. It was wrong and made me feel terrible. Chasing after someone who doesn't want you is a terrible feeling. I'm actively trying to change that mindset, moving from feeling like good things are rare to respecting myself more. I promise myself I'll never do that again.

As I mark the end of Day 3, I'm pleased with my progress, estimating myself to be at around 20% of the healing process. There's so much to look forward to as I continue on this journey. Keep up the good work!

Day 4:

Today, I had a tough time trying to feel better. When I woke up in the middle of the night, I couldn't stop thinking about him. I remembered all the good times we had, how special our relationship was, and how we faced challenges together. Thinking about how we both grew and achieved our dreams together makes me sad now that we're not together anymore. Even though we used to be close, it's hard to accept that we're now practically strangers. To put it simply, I really miss him. Even though I try to think about other things, I can't stop thinking about him. Is it normal to feel this way while trying to heal? It hurts to think about him being happy with someone else, like he doesn't care about our past. I wonder if she's lucky to have him, or if she'll end up feeling as sad as I do. Even though he's with someone new, he still comes to see me and spends nights with me. I wonder if he loves her more, me more, or maybe just himself more than anyone else.

Even though I really want him to be happy with me, I know it wouldn't be right to force him to love me. I feel sad, but I'm trying hard to move forward. Is there a way to stop feeling heartbroken? They say time heals, but without accepting what's happened, the pain just sticks around forever. So, I'm focusing on accepting things now. Maybe our paths are meant to go different ways, and he's supposed to be with someone else, just like I might find someone else too. Maybe this is the end of our story, and I need to think about starting a new one. Even though I'm not completely sure, I know this is the right thing to do. I hope he finds true happiness, and I'll try to be happy too, even though it might take a while. Healing isn't easy, but I'm going to keep trying every day.

I wonder if he thinks about me like I think about him. Or maybe he's moved on and is happy with someone else. Does he think about getting back together? But dwelling on these thoughts only hinders my progress. So instead, I'm focusing on improving myself. I believe that one day, I'll emerge stronger because of this experience.

Day 5:

Lately, I've been feeling really anxious, like I can't breathe and my chest might burst. Even though I try, I can't stop thinking about him, and it's hard not to get stuck on those thoughts. I feel like crying, but the tears won't come. Today has been tough, but I'm trying to stay focused. Fortunately, I was able to concentrate. I recently joined a Toastmaster club and participated in an international speech competition. The theme was "You are valuable," and I'm happy that the audience appreciated my speech.

Receiving positive feedback from my fellow Toastmasters felt really good, especially because many of them connected deeply with my speech. It's somewhat surprising how people I don't even know can recognize my value, appreciate me, and feel fortunate to have met me. That day, I decided to change how I see things. I realized I shouldn't waste my energy on things that aren't important. Instead of feeling bad about someone who doesn't deserve it, I'm writing in a journal about my feelings, and it's been making me feel better. I know it will take time to feel better, but I believe I'm making progress.

Right now, I'm working my part-time job, even though it's my day off. This job isn't just about money for me; it also gives me emotional support. Seeing my trainees respect and appreciate me has changed how I see myself, reminding me that I'm valuable. I've decided to stop dwelling on thoughts of him, take some time to rest, and focus on my other work as well.

To lift my spirits, my cousin and I are going to the salon for some self-care. It's important to take care of myself, be kind to myself, and focus on self-love. I deserve this treat, and it helps me relax a lot. Even though today was tough, I'm proud of how I handled it. I wanted to check his status on WhatsApp and reinstall my social media apps, but I resisted the temptation. I plan to keep it up and promise myself I'll only go back to social media when I'm feeling better, trusting that things will get better with time and with God's help.

Day 6:

Hey there! I nearly reinstalled my Instagram and TikTok apps because I wanted to check on him, but I stopped myself and exercised self-control. Even though I still think about him sometimes, it's not as strong as it used to be. Today, I kept busy by chatting with my family back in the Philippines—my mom, sisters, brothers, cousins—and it felt really good. It's important to stay in touch with loved ones while you're healing; they can help you see things differently.

I said no to the two guys who asked me out because I'm not ready to date right now. Despite declining their offers, they're still pursuing me, and a friend suggested they see it as a challenge. I'm not saying no forever, but I'm also not ready to think about dating. If they're still interested when I am ready, then we'll see who's the best fit. Right now, I'm focused on studying for the PMP course, which took a lot of hard work over five weeks. It paid off—I passed the exam! My IMC relationship manager congratulated me and told me I can download my PMP Certificate in three days. It really made my day to achieve this.

Furthermore, I have arranged a meeting with my potential business partners to discuss investment opportunities and potentially sign a six-month contract. This is another good thing happening for me. As many people know, going through heartache can help you grow. Now, I can focus on my goals and work hard to reach them. Even though the pain is still there, I know it's not good to stay stuck in it forever. I trust that in due time, God will bring someone into my life who will love and respect me as I deserve.

I have a date planned with a guy, but I've informed him that we can only be friends as I'm currently too busy for anything more. I want to keep moving forward without any distractions. It wouldn't be fair to start a new relationship when I'm not ready. I said 'Yes' to the date because he's already planned it, but I'm bringing my cousin with me. It's okay to meet new people, but it's important to take time to heal before starting something new.

Day 7:

Today has been extremely busy, with back-to-back meetings from 9:30 AM until 5:00 PM. However, the positive side is that I haven't been thinking about him much. Being busy can be beneficial if you're using it for self-development and improvement rather than just as an escape. It helps to focus on your goals and objectives, leaving little time for dwelling on unimportant matters. I've also stopped expecting his calls or messages. I'd say I'm about 30% okay on my healing journey. I don't want to rush things, but consistency is key. Even though I was tempted to reinstall my social media, I resisted and maintained self-control..

Being consistent is really important. Even though the pain persists, I feel lucky to have gradually moved from that tough situation. I'm proud of myself for being able to live without seeing him, talking to him, or messaging him. In the past, if he didn't message me or check up on me for three days, I'd get really anxious and think the worst, like maybe he found someone else and forgot about me. I used to be the one to call him if I hadn't heard from him, and I'd feel relieved when I heard his voice again. I know it's not healthy, and it seems like I have attachment issues, but adhering to the "no contact rule" is helping me gradually detach from him.

I once read an article about how to move on from somebody. The author stated you cannot move on from somebody until you detach from them, and you can't detach from them without realizing that you were attached to them. I think the key questions to ask are: 'Why am I attached to this person, and what void do I believe they are filling within me?' If it's because they validated me and made me feel loved, it indicates that I don't love myself enough. If you truly love yourself, you won't depend on others for love. Every person you're with reflects something within you. So, if you struggle with something in a relationship, it's likely because you struggle with that aspect of yourself, and they're reflecting it back to you. Realizing this helps shift the focus away from them and onto yourself.

Truly, awakening occurs when hitting rock bottom with a person makes you realize your true value and deserving of something better. Letting go and moving on become easier because you see things more clearly. I'm glad I've consistently survived Day 7.

Day 8:

Feeling overwhelmed today, I'm proud to have finally received my PMP Certificate. Achieving this milestone required dedication, intensive study, and passing the exam. This accomplishment marks a significant turning point in my corporate ladder. I attribute my success to maintaining focus, isolating myself from the distractions of social media, and eliminating the obstacles that hindered my progress.

Looking back on what's been happening lately, I've noticed that when I get stressed, especially during conflicts, I tend to reach for a cigarette without even thinking about it. Even though some people might say it's not true, I know it helps me deal with things. But ever since I started on my journey to heal and began fasting, I've found that I can think more clearly and I'm better at not giving in to the urge to smoke. This shows me that if I can control what I eat, I can also control other parts of my life.

Fasting has helped me think clearly and make smart choices. I've realized that moving on was the best thing for me. I don't regret it at all, and I know I deserve more than just scraps in relationships. Knowing my own value has given me the strength to break free from being treated badly in past relationships.

Even though I still think about him sometimes, it doesn't hurt anymore. My goal is to get to a place where thoughts of him don't affect me at all. I know I'm not perfect, and I've made mistakes in the relationship, but I also know I'm valuable. I know I messed up and I really need to fix my old hurts because they're bothering me and maybe causing problems for him too. Sometimes, I acted really crazy, but he stayed patient with me. When I accused him of something, he tried to explain, even though he didn't have to. I admit I'm not perfect and it hurts my confidence. That's why I want to improve, not just for him, but for myself, like he always told me to do that.

From this experience, I've learned how crucial it is to keep being myself in a relationship, to love myself first, and not to be too controlling. It's important to give each other room to grow and not rely completely on someone else for happiness. As I continue to heal, I'm staying focused on getting better. On Day 8 of my journey, I'm still not using social media, and I'm putting my energy into moving on and thinking about what comes next, step by step.

Day 9:

I still find myself thinking about him, especially before I go to sleep and when I wake up, which I think is normal while I'm trying to heal. But during the day, when I'm busy with work and other activities, I hardly think about him, which shows that I'm making progress on my healing journey. By being alone, staying away from social media, and not contacting him, I've been able to heal considerably. Not only are my feelings getting better, but I'm also feeling mentally and physically healthier.

I've stopped smoking, started exercising regularly, improved my diet, and I sleep better because my mind is more peaceful.

Although thoughts of him still pop up from time to time, they don't take over my mind the way they used to. Before, I was obsessed, filled with anxiety, and couldn't shake off intrusive thoughts. But on my ninth day of healing, I'm proud of how far I've come. It feels like a sudden change, realizing how important self-respect is. It's crucial not to let someone else's actions harm your mental health. Having self-respect means knowing when to walk away if someone doesn't feel right. Even though he left me hurt, it's actually made me feel better about myself. I'm starting to accept what's happened and focusing on my own growth and goals, which I'm really excited about achieving.

Letting go of expectations and focusing on improving myself has felt freeing. I've stopped imagining a future with us and genuinely want him to be happy, no matter what he chooses. Before, I was scared of being alone, but now am enjoying being alone. I deserve love and care, and I deserve to be someone's first choice, not just one of many options. I also understand that if you have to chase someone, they're probably not the right person for you. When it's real love, there's no need for chasing or forcing things. Love should feel easy, not heavy.

Despite the heartbreaks I've experienced in the past, I still believe in love and hold onto optimism. I don't harbor any bitterness and have faith that the right person will come into my life at the right time. For now, my main focus is on healing myself. I want to ensure that when I do meet someone new, I'll be emotionally whole and free from all my past trauma or anxiety. In fact, I no longer experience anxiety attacks; they're a thing of the past. This shows that I'm making progress until the pain fades away completely, and his presence or absence no longer affects me. My life is moving forward, and I'm embracing it.

Day 10:

I'm halfway through my healing journey, and I've reached a point where I can accept everything that's happened. I'm also forgiving myself for letting others mistreat me and not valuing myself enough, especially in my past relationships that really caused me so much trauma, which affected my relationship with my previous partner. After all, if I didn't respect myself, how could I expect anyone else to? That's why the healing process feels easier this time around. I've found clarity by isolating myself from social media, focusing on myself, feeding my mind with positive things, and working towards my long-term goals. These steps have been effective in helping me heal.

Sadness and loneliness still visit me, but I know those feelings won't last forever. Surprisingly, I hardly think about him anymore, and mentally, it's been really good for me. Instead of overthinking, I'm focusing my energy on what's important. Writing has become a big part of my healing process. It allows me to express myself without fear of judgment. Every day, I'm feeling a little bit better, and I'm looking forward to where this journey takes me. I'm excited to share my experiences with others who are going through similar struggles of letting go of the wrong people.

The key I've discovered is valuing yourself enough to not let anyone treat you the way you didn't deserve. Reminding myself of this every day helps reinforce how important I am. I'm not afraid of being alone; in fact, I'm enjoying my single life. I'm slowly healing, and I'm no longer fixated on anyone or anything. There are still plenty of days ahead on this healing journey, but I'm confident I'll get there. I'm just focusing on loving myself more and more because I owe that to myself, and no one else can do it for me.

I'm happy that I've been sticking to my plans, and it's paying off. Maybe I should have started earlier, but it's okay; it's never too late. This could be the right time for me to move on, to heal, and to focus on myself as I have neglected myself for years just to please my ex-partners in the past. Life is valuable, and we shouldn't waste it on someone who doesn't appreciate us. From now on, I'll prioritize myself, never settling for less and never letting anyone treat me poorly. I regret letting someone disrespect me, but I won't allow it to happen again. I'll always take care of myself, and if a relationship doesn't bring me peace or make me feel valued, I'll gracefully leave. It's normal to feel angry during the healing process, but I'll work through it until I truly forgive myself so I can finally heal from my childhood traumas and other traumas I had in my first and second relationships. Mostly, I am overcoming the traumas they caused me, and I am working on it.

Day 11:

Moving on can be a challenging journey. Although I believed I was making progress, I unexpectedly found myself feeling angry and sad. Thoughts of him consumed much of my day, and it dawned on me that I still had photos of him in my phone gallery. Despite lacking the courage to delete our shared memories, I realized it was necessary for my healing but I really couldn't. I'm allowed myself to feel the pain, acknowledging that it's a crucial part of the process. Although I considered reaching out to him, I'm relieved I didn't. After all, why should I chase someone who chose to leave me for someone else? I know moving on is really hard but knowing my worth, value and self-respect would make my decision right.

While moving on is difficult, I understand the importance of recognizing my self-worth and refusing to settle for less. I refuse to accept mere morsels of attention or affection, as I know what I bring to the table. I'm prepared to reciprocate effort, love, and care with those who appreciate me. I refuse to be anyone's second choice or backup plan—I am the prize. I am closing the door on any possibility of reconciliation, as I refuse to be manipulated or treated any less than I deserve.

Day 12:

This morning, I felt lighter and more relaxed when I woke up, like a big weight had been taken off me. It was a pleasant surprise to sleep so soundly, and for once, he didn't bother my dreams or fill my mind. I can say with certainty that I'm moving forward, and I'm committed to not dwelling on the past. When he called and messaged me today, I decided not to reply right away. In the past, I'd always respond even when I was busy, but now I'm trying to put work first and message him whenever I am free.

I'm okay now. I'm focusing on my goals and striving to become a better version of myself. I've set my standards and boundaries, and I'm sticking to them. I've learned my lessons, and accepting breadcrumbs is no longer an option for me. I'm done with this situation, and I deserve better.

I'm proud of myself for resisting the urge to respond to his calls and messages because it shows that I'm making progress. By isolating myself from the world of social media and implementing the strict 'No Contact' rule, I've been able to move on and heal consistently. I've also come to realize that the rule can lead to two different outcomes: either realizing one's worth and refusing to settle for less, or feeling a lot of regret. And I'm determined to be on the side of realizing my worth and never settling for anything less than I deserve.

Random Thoughts of Healing

Day 13:

He rang me again last night. I felt the need to gauge my reaction if I were to pick up his call. Don't judge me for ultimately answering. We conversed, catching up and exchanging life updates. Despite expecting to feel anger, surprisingly, I didn't. The fond memories we shared and his role in shaping my life outweighed any negative emotions. We cleared up misunderstandings from our previous conversations before this period of isolation, which left us feeling better. I experienced relief and found myself accepting everything more deeply. He reassured me of my significance to him, and I reciprocated the sentiment. This time, it felt genuine. We agreed to maintain a friendship with defined boundaries. I'd say I'm halfway through my healing journey, feeling lighter than before. I've stopped fantasizing about a romantic future with him, redirecting my focus toward personal goals.

Anger is a natural stage of healing, but as reality and clarity set in, things improve. I thought reconnecting with him might alter my decision, but it didn't. I reiterated to him that I'm committed to moving forward, unwilling to remain stuck in the same cycle. I'm embracing the 'it is what it is' mentality, believing that if things are meant to be, they'll unfold regardless of circumstances. I sense a profound shift since our conversation. My understanding and emotional maturity have grown, even prompting a friend to suggest I start a podcast to share my experiences and advice on relationships, moving on, and healing. I've gained a comprehensive understanding of self-respect, self-love, and self-care. I can discern between desperation and genuine aspiration, realizing that we can only control our emotions, not others or external circumstances.

Life becomes simpler when we release our attachment to outcomes and refrain from overthinking the future. I am happy with my decision, and I am proud of my progress.

Day 14:

Today, I spent time with my family at the zoo, and though it might seem like a simple outing, I found joy in it, especially surrounded by nature. Nature has a remarkable ability to reset our minds and provide solace when we're feeling down, stressed, or upset. Being immersed in nature can have a profound impact on our emotional well-being, acting as a tonic for our mental health. It can lower blood pressure, stabilize heart rate, and reduce the production of stress hormones. Experts often recommend spending time at the beach or in any natural setting when feeling low, and I've personally found it to be highly effective.

Despite reconnecting with him after two weeks, my resolve remains unchanged, and I'm fully committed to completing my healing journey. I've stopped fantasizing about a future with him; instead, I'm focused on moving forward, which is immensely freeing. While I still experience moments of sadness and loneliness, I recognize these emotions as valid parts of the healing process. I'm taking things slow, allowing myself to feel all emotions because they're essential for true healing.

I firmly believe in my own worth and refuse to rush back into the dating scene. Currently, the only social media platform I use is LinkedIn, which I find beneficial for my well-being. Though I used to share my achievements and events on social media, I've decided to keep them private for now. My priority is achieving my goals and achieving complete healing before considering rejoining social media or entertaining the idea of a new relationship.

I've turned down three guys who showed interest in me, telling them I'm not ready for anything more and it wouldn't be fair to them. I believe in being honest and prefer to be clear. I won't lean on anyone to ease my sadness or loneliness; I'm focused on healing in my own way and at my own pace.

Just as going grocery shopping on an empty stomach leads to poor decisions, entering a relationship out of loneliness can result in choosing the wrong person. It's crucial to approach relationships from a place of emotional stability and self-assurance rather than seeking validation from others.

Day 15:

Today, I'm feeling down. It's like sadness is covering everything, and I'm struggling with feeling alone. I've always been the type to talk things out, sharing my day with someone who cares. I miss having that with him. He used to tease me about talking so much but was always there to listen. I miss him, but I'm sticking to my decision to move on. I'm focused on healing, more determined than ever.

It feels like a repeating pattern: I try to move forward, but when he contacts me, I'm back where I started. He's not a bad person in fact he is my hero; maybe it's just not our time yet. Looking back on his impact on my life after my last relationship, I'm thankful. Even though I feel sad today, I know tomorrow could be different. Emotions go up and down, and I'm accepting this healing journey, even though it's hard. I believe it will make me stronger in the end.

To take my mind off things, I went to the park and spent time walking and running. I'm working on not thinking about him so much, as he's been on my mind a lot lately. We've already said our thoughts and ended things on good terms in our last talk. I've set rules and expectations, and he's respected them. One of the toughest parts of healing is changing habits, like not talking to him or seeing him every weekend. But that's how life goes; people move in and out of our lives, and it's important not to get too attached.

I'm proud of sticking to my decision. I've kept social media apps uninstalled and am in the process of detachment. There's no lingering anger, and I've stopped fantasizing about us. I'm halfway through my healing journey, and though it's slow, I'm satisfied with my progress. I'm taking my time, focusing on myself. There are aspects I need to work on, like facing and healing from childhood traumas. This is a season of self-improvement, preparing myself emotionally, mentally, and physically for the right person when they come along. I refuse to repeat past mistakes; I've learned to love myself above all else, shedding insecurities and obsessions from previous relationships.

I look forward to the day when I become the best version of myself. I anticipate the wonderful transition ahead of me with eager anticipation.

Day 16:

Last night, he reached out with an "Eid Mubarak" greeting, a customary exchange between fellow Muslims. Our conversation was brief, and I noticed a shift within myself—I no longer felt the excitement that once accompanied his messages. Surprisingly, this realization didn't bother me; it simply meant that he no longer held sway over my emotions and had become just another person in my life.

Thinking back on a talk with a friend about my ex's hesitation to commit or get married, I found it hard to explain why I wanted marriage with him. Even though he has some good qualities, I really want a partner who stands by me, especially since I'm a single mom. While I've always cared about him a lot, I've also wished to be cared for in return.

Today feels lighter; the weight of 'what ifs' has lifted, and I find peace of mind. My thoughts seldom wander to him, maybe because I'm preoccupied with preparing for an upcoming event where I'll be hosting. Shopping is a therapeutic activity that brings me immense joy. It is important to find personal avenues for stress relief, rather than relying on others for dopamine hits. Currently, I'm finding solace within myself, and it's proven to be remarkably effective, especially during my healing journey.

I'm grateful to God, as prayers are being answered, and the pain is gradually subsiding. While I cherish the memories we shared, I'm beginning to detach myself from him, trusting that the universe will guide us both. Whether our paths converge again remains uncertain, but for now, I'm relishing in my newfound singlehood and the peace it brings. One day, when the time is right, I'll be open to whoever is meant for me.

Day 17:

Today, I hardly thought about him, which suggests significant progress and genuine healing on my part. I can confidently say that I'm doing well and I've come to accept our situation, which has brought me a profound sense of peace. My sleep has improved remarkably, and I've successfully quit the habit of smoking since the very first day I decided to move on and heal. I haven't reinstalled all my social media apps yet. I've stopped checking his WhatsApp status, and I haven't initiated any calls or texts. I'm living my life independently now. Besides focusing on healing, I'm actively addressing my abandonment and attachment issues through meditation and exercise. I'm

Random Thoughts of Healing

keeping myself busy with meaningful activities every day. Maintaining a journal has also contributed to my overall improvement. While the healing process may evoke sadness, I recognize its essential role in fostering personal growth. They say, "There's no gain without pain," and I'm willing to endure the pain if it means long-term improvement.

Today, we went to the movies and watched "Kung Fu Panda 4" with my family. We had a great time, and the movie offered valuable life lessons. One lesson that stuck with me is that "Change is scary, but it's worth it." It may feel uncomfortable at first as we're accustomed to what's familiar, but it's important to give new experiences a chance. I'm open to meeting new people, although I'm not rushing into relationships. Entertaining others allows me to practice the lessons I've learned from past experiences. I have firm standards and boundaries, and I'm honest with anyone who doesn't meet them. It's better to be blunt than to give false hope, as I don't want to waste time on relationships with no future. Right now, I'm focused on healing alone and not using someone else as a rebound. Being single has its advantages, giving me ample time to reflect on my past and set high standards to protect myself in future relationships. Healing may take time, but it's a priority for me before committing to anything else.

Overall, I'm content with my progress and consistency, and I'm genuinely in a better place now.

Day 18:

Today was fantastic for me; I even rekindled my love for music after a hiatus, and I've truly missed that light, serene feeling where everything just falls into place. Surprisingly, thoughts of him scarcely crossed my mind, and I felt a lot more positive compared to previous days. It's safe to say I'm gradually improving and I am 60% through my healing process. My journey to healing isn't a straight path; it's about accepting bad days as they come and not rushing the process. I'm taking it slow, embracing the pain, sadness, and loneliness, knowing it'll lead to long-term growth. This healing process is crucial for me; I refuse to fall back into the cycle of questioning my self-worth ever again, especially after the setbacks in my past relationships. Despite the heartache, I've learned valuable lessons and I'm confronting my past traumas head-on, acknowledging my abandonment and attachment issues.

Detachment is key to moving forward, and I'm actively working on my issues, eager for long-term progress. While relapses may occur, I'm better equipped to handle my emotions now. I've mastered emotional control and constantly ask myself if someone adds value to my life and if I truly want to be with them. I'm becoming more confident in my self-worth and can accept his decision, even if he's with someone else. Frankly, I no longer dwell on it; his choices no longer weigh on me, and I'm grateful for the peace of mind. I'm proud of my consistency during this healing journey; it's been effective because I've realized I deserve more and won't settle for less. I'm focused on self-love, improving myself mentally, physically, and emotionally.

Setting high standards isn't about being selfish; it's about safeguarding myself and making wise choices for the future. No more repeating past mistakes - I won't beg, force, or chase anyone. I'll only welcome someone into my life if they genuinely want me, choose me, and prioritize me. I will only exert my valuable time and effort for someone who is reciprocating my feelings and attention. I will never give my 100% best anymore to someone doesn't deserve me, especially someone who is not ready for any kind of commitment. I don't want to feel unwanted, undervalued, or like an option anymore. Lastly, I refuse to question my value or wonder if there's something wrong with me. I am completely free from a victim mindset.

Day 19:

Last night, peace eluded me. Thoughts of him flooded my mind, his presence lingering in the quiet of the night. It felt like he was reaching out, calling for a connection that I too felt drawn to. Despite the temptation, I managed to resist. However, tears fell for the emptiness his absence left behind. My home, once filled with our shared moments, now felt haunted by memories of him. Every corner reminded me of his visits, his warmth, his laughter—all of it. Though I yearn for him, I know that returning to that cycle of pain isn't the answer, as those days are gone. I've come to accept that our paths may lead in different directions for now. Perhaps he's meant for someone else, and I'm for another. This realization, though sad, brings a sense of peace, relieving the constant uncertainty.

To distract myself, I threw myself into household chores. Cleaning and cooking provided temporary solace, a momentary escape from my thoughts. Seeing the tangible results—a tidy home and delicious meals— brought a fleeting sense of contentment. Just as I was about to rest, I noticed his missed calls and messages on my phone. He had stopped by the garage near my place and expressed a desire to visit. I called him back, and we ended up talking for hours, catching up on life. It was one of the things I missed about him—our easy comfort with each other. However, this time, talking to him felt different. Instead of the hopeful anticipation I used to feel, there was mutual acceptance.

As mentioned before, acceptance and letting go are key to healing and moving on. It felt good to let go of hate and negative thoughts. Talking to him didn't change my mind; I'm still eager to heal completely. I'm focusing on myself and ticking off items on my bucket list. I look forward to the day when I'm fully healed, not just from him, but also from past traumas deep within.

Day 20:

Today was busy, keeping me fully occupied and pulling my thoughts away from him. I had the chance to meet truly remarkable individuals—gifted public speakers—who left me feeling inspired. Their presence motivated me, and I aspire to develop my skills to become an exceptional public speaker myself. Exploring my passions and stepping outside my comfort zone are all part of my healing process. Instead of dwelling on sadness, I'm embracing new interests and pursuits. The chapter of sorrow is behind me now, and I'm grateful for the peace I've found. Pain, obsession, overthinking, and fantasies no longer dominate my thoughts.

Despite feeling tired today, the positive feedback I received for my hosting lifted my spirits. It's true what they say—sometimes, breakups bring unexpected blessings. I decided to reinstall social media as a way to share my achievements, seeing it as a sign of progress. Importantly, I resisted the urge to check his profile, which was a healthy choice. My posts were driven by personal growth, not a desire for his attention. However, I soon realized that social media could easily distract me from more meaningful activities like journaling and working on my book. So, I made the decision to opt out, recognizing it as a hindrance to my progress.

I'd say I'm about 60% healed, with ongoing efforts to reach full recovery. Each day brings new challenges and victories, but I'm determined to keep moving forward.

Day 21.

It all boils down to your mindset. Embrace the journey of self-care, deep healing, and self-improvement with patience, compassion, and respect for your own path. Understand that feelings of being stuck or sadness stem from the power of our minds. But remember, it's never too late to change our habits, our outlook, and ultimately, ourselves. Let go of relationships that only offer bare minimum, and recognize that clinging to someone who doesn't value you is a sign of lacking self-respect. My own healing journey has become easier now that I've recognized my self-worth. Life is full of opportunities, and while it may take time, trust in your own journey and destiny. Instead of dwelling on past relationships, focus on the possibility that they're making room for someone better suited for you. These realizations have transformed my outlook, leaving me feeling invigorated, purposeful, and content. Today, despite a busy workday, thoughts of him didn't even cross my mind as they once did.

  He'll always hold a special place in my heart, and I'll forever cherish the memories we shared. He played a significant role in my life, especially during those tough times when I needed guidance. He was my rock, lending an ear whenever I needed someone to talk to. We were there for each other through thick and thin, supporting one another as we navigated through past relationships and sought solace in each other's company. Perhaps our paths diverged for now, but who's to say what the future holds? I've stopped stressing over what might come to pass and instead focus on the present moment. I've made strides in improving myself, starting with breaking the habit of smoking and dedicating time to nourish my mind with books and my body through exercise. I've learned to let go of overthinking and find peace within myself. No longer do I seek validation from others; if my presence isn't appreciated, I gracefully step aside. Life's complexities are often of our own making, and I've embraced simplicity. I'm proud of the person I'm becoming and remain committed to continual self-improvement.

So believe me when I say that setting the proper mindset helps me to heal. Our brain is so powerful, which is why we can always rebuke all the negative thoughts and replace them with our self-affirmation. I always believe that I am valuable and I am the prize, I am beautiful, I am unique and I am authentic. It really gives me peace of mind, relief and self-satisfaction. Proper detachment plays an effective role in healing too; it makes you see things clearer, see issues from a bird's eye view. It's a balance between perspective and presence that makes us successful in healing for doing the right thing for ourselves. Keep going until you reach the destination with a strong foundation.

Day 22.

It was raining the whole day, and childhood memories came back to me, making me feel happy, stress-free, and with taste of freedom and peace. I was also productive the whole day, from back to back meeting, and there was a one-on-one meeting that we were supposed to discuss, but we ended up sharing interesting stories of our lives. I was glad that I talked to her, and I could feel that both of us were on the same wavelength and the same mindset. It feels good when you are sharing your experiences with someone who appreciates your thoughts and opinions.

Meeting new people with the same mindset is one of the keys to purposeful healing, especially if you are leaving an impact on someone's life. That's why it is recommended that you go out and meet new people and build new connections that will help you change your perspective and mindset. We may have time just to lie down on our bed because we really need to attend to our emotions and deal with them. Feel the pain, embrace the brokenness, be mad, be sad; however, you should know when to stop.

I feel great and happy with my healing journey. I haven't felt any kind of pain today at all. I haven't considered the possibility that he might be with someone else and happy. Besides, I often find myself asking: "What drives my desire for these experiences?" "Why do I seek neglect?" "Why do I tolerate mistreatment?" "Why do I want someone who is not willing to commit with me?" "Why do I need someone who doesn't have any value in my life?" "Why do I want someone who lets me feel unimportant?" "Why do I need someone who can't prioritize me?" "Why do I want someone who can't choose me?" "Why do I need someone who gives me little attention?" "Why do I want someone who doesn't care?" "Why do I need someone who doesn't love me?" Yes, I keep asking these questions repeatedly because they help me maintain self-control, while also nurturing my sense of self-worth, respect, and love. They serve as pillars in my healing journey, fortifying my resolve. I maintain a steadfast belief that someone will be there for me, perhaps not now, but when the timing is right. This internal dialogue proves invaluable. No longer do I linger in sadness or brokenness; instead, I wholeheartedly welcome a newfound sense of wholeness and contentment, even in solitude. I've learned to find happiness within myself, no longer seeking validation or attention from others. Thus, I can confidently assert that my journey towards healing progresses steadily through consistency and perseverance.

Day 23:

I'm surprised I didn't think about him today. I didn't think I could move on from him, but it seems I have. I've stopped waiting for his calls or messages, I've stopped checking on him on all social media platforms, I've stopped doing all those crazy things, I've stopped invading his privacy as he always warned me that it would make me look miserable. Maybe he cared about me, but there are things we cannot force to happen.

It's true that one sign of healing from someone is when their presence or absence no longer affects you. Being consistent and exercising self-control helped me move forward. I've detached myself from him and the situation, trying to understand what initially drew me in. I'm glad I can manage my emotions now; I don't feel any pain. However, I'm not entirely sure if I'm completely healed yet. Healing can sometimes come with setbacks. Today, I feel fine, but tomorrow might bring something different. What matters most is that I recognize my worth and respect myself. I feel light and peaceful, staying focusing on my goals.

Recently, I launched an Instagram page where I share thoughts on healing, hoping to inspire others. My aim is to grow a following and potentially monetize it in the future. Concurrently, I'm also working on a book, with a target to compete it within 90 days. I'm enthusiastic about my future achievements and confident that moving on was the right decision. Breakups can indeed be blessings in disguise, fostering strength and altering perspectives. I'd say I'm about 70% healed now.

I've stopped worrying about whether he's talking to or dating someone else; it's simply not worth my time and energy. Instead, I focus on activities like writing, reading, and exercising, which nourish both my mind and body. Today marks day 23 of my healing journey, and I'm maintaining consistency with productive pursuits.

Day 24:

I feel overwhelmed and really happy today. I'm making great progress this time. I didn't even think about him; I was busy at work and working on my Instagram page, sharing some thoughts on healing that I've gathered and experienced. Before, I didn't want to stop feeling anything for him. I didn't want him to just become like any other person to me. I didn't want to

Random Thoughts of Healing

forget about him or move on. But I've realized that you don't have to forget someone or erase all the good memories you've shared because a truly healed person knows how to appreciate someone who has meant a lot to them.

I feel calm now. Before, I tried to find peace, but I couldn't. I feel grateful that I met him. He's been a part of my successes. Maybe I'm feeling this way because a lot of good things have happened to me lately as I've been healing and moving forward. I used to think he was my only source of happiness, and I was scared of losing him. But now I know there are many ways to be happy without relying on one person. I still want someone special in my life, but I've learned that kindness, even in small ways, can bring happiness too.

I saw a friend's Instagram post where she seemed torn between waiting for someone and forgetting about them. It reminded me of my own struggles with moving on, so I replied to her post, saying she should always prioritize herself and learn to let go. I told her that detaching from a person or situation can lead to two outcomes: either they realize your worth and come back, or you realize your own worth and decide you don't need them. Either way, you win. Surprisingly, she responded happily and seemed to change her outlook. She even followed my page and liked all my posts. It felt great to connect with her and share my experiences. She supports my page because she appreciates my efforts to spread love and wisdom to others going through similar struggles. I just want to help others with the healing journey I've been on.

The key is to find happiness within ourselves instead of relying on others. There are plenty of things that can bring us joy, like being kind, sharing wisdom, meeting new people, chatting with loved ones, and working towards our goals. Happiness shouldn't be dependent on anyone; it's something we should create for ourselves through various experiences and actions.

Day 25:

I'm grateful for everything, even as I continue to heal. This journey seems to be guiding me toward where I need to be. It's reignited my passion to finish my book and pursue activities that bring me joy. Lately, I launched an Instagram page where I share random thoughts on healing. I'm thrilled to post inspirational quotes and uplift others. It feels like my way of offering support, especially to those facing tough times. The positive feedback I've received is really motivating me to keep pushing forward.

On the healing front, I'm making good progress. He reached out, worried that my new page on heartbreak might trigger painful memories. Surprisingly, I reassured him that starting the page actually brought me relief and happiness. It's made me super enthusiastic and driven to create content and work on my book all day.

In my daily journal, I always remind myself that healing takes dedication and consistency. Moving on means sticking to your decision and having the courage to let go of anything that doesn't bring peace. I've found comfort in the notion that 'Whatever is meant to be, will be.' Letting go of worry has really brought me peace.

As for him, I no longer hold onto anger like I did in the early days of my healing journey. It's natural to feel hurt when we're not chosen, but I've come to realize that it's a reflection of our own self-respect and self-worth. I've finally unlocked the key to moving on, which I've discovered is truly loving yourself and never settling for less.

Day 26:

Lately, I've found solace in organizing, decluttering, tackling household chores, and whipping up meals – they've become my go-to therapies on this healing journey. I'm truly grateful to see how progress I've made this time around. I've even dusted off my old habit of playing music, which gives me a refreshing energy boost. It's quite a shift from before when the mere sound of music would stir up my sadness. This progress indicates that I'm not only healing from him but also from the childhood traumas I've endured.

To confront these challenges, I've turned to meditation, self-forgiveness, and acknowledging my past mistreatment. This chapter of my life is all about putting myself first — indulging in things that bring me joy, treating myself to items I've denied myself before, and pampering myself with salon visits and self-love practices. I recognize the importance of being fully healed before stepping into any new relationship.

Luckily, I'm in no rush because I'm relishing my time alone. I've found peace of mind, freedom, and the liberty to pursue whatever brings me happiness.

Initially, the healing journey can be tough. There are ups and downs, good days, and bad days, but I believe it's all part of the process. As I've mentioned before, consistency is key – stick to your decisions and avoid dwelling on the past. A healed individual naturally attracts other healed souls, and I refuse to settle for someone who hasn't yet undergone their own growth and maturity. A wise friend once told me that mature men appreciate women like me, so that's where my focus lies at the moment. I genuinely feel that I've moved on from my ex this time, and I'm fully committed to my personal growth and maturity.

I'd estimate I'm about 80% along in my healing journey, and I'm eager to continue evolving into the best version of myself. .

Day 27:

I've come to realize that dedicating 30 days to my healing journey has truly made a difference in overcoming the traumas from my past relationships. Engaging in healing activities has been instrumental, and now, if I were to meet someone new or enter another relationship, I wouldn't carry the same paranoia or obsession as before. This journey has bolstered my self-confidence as I've recognized my own value and worth.

Random Thoughts of Healing

I've also come to understand that this healing journey isn't solely about my most recent relationship; it's about confronting the traumas from my past relationships that I've been avoiding. Previously, I tended to evade facing my fears, but now I grasp the importance of sitting with and processing all my emotions. It's important to allow ourselves to experience everything until it becomes more manageable. Ignoring these traumas could potentially harm any future relationships we pursue.

Today, I'm feeling deeply happy and fulfilled, which shows that I'm making real progress in my healing journey. I'm eager to continue evolving into the best version of myself and to keep growing further.

Day 28:

The day was remarkably calm, and I felt deeply touched by the support pouring in from my coworkers, family, and friends. I'm truly feeling okay now. There's no more room for hate, grudges, or sadness in my heart. I've made peace with everyone who hurt me before, and most importantly, I've forgiven myself. Forgiving yourself is a significant part of healing. You need to forgive yourself for letting people treat you badly in the past.

Instead of dwelling on the past, we should be grateful for the lessons we've learned from pain and suffering. Tough times make us stronger and wiser. We can use that pain to transform our lives for the better. It's important to use pain as a guide to set boundaries and standards for ourselves, so we never find ourselves in such tough situations again.

Today, I feel profoundly grateful because I realize that I wouldn't be able to share my beliefs and passions with others if I hadn't overcome the traumas and challenges I faced in the past. I'm grateful for the person I've become today. Surprisingly, I'm even thankful for those who caused me pain, because their actions helped shape me into who I am now, in a much better place.

Day 29:

Wow, I'm so amazed by how far I've come on my healing journey. It all began with me finding the courage to change my thinking and decisions. I have no regrets about it. I feel like I'm getting closer to being fully healed from the tough times I've been through. Now, I understand what made me cling to others for validation, but I'm not seeking that anymore. The best part is, I'm learning to love and take care of myself like never before. It's like I'm finally giving myself the attention and care I deserve.

Right now, I'm really enjoying my own company, and I don't think I'll ever be scared of being alone again, just in case. My main focus is on reaching my goals. I've got five big goals in mind, and I've already achieved two of them. But I still have three left on my list that need my dedication and attention. This is one of the great things about healing. When you're healed, you can focus on whatever you want to achieve in your life because all your attention is on yourself, not on anyone else. That's why they call this stage "Me, Myself, and I". It's all about taking care of yourself and going after your dreams. This time, I am chasing my dreams and not chasing or forcing love or relationships.

Day 30:

This is my journey. I've set aside 30 days to heal and move forward, not just from my last relationship, but also from the pain and trauma I've carried for so long. In the past, I struggled with insecurity, lacked confidence, and was filled with self-doubt. I used to overthink everything, dwell on past mistakes, and felt like a victim of circumstances. Trust was hard for me, and I often saw the world through a negative lens.

But today, things are different. I've transformed. I've become more focused on my goals and less focused on others. I've worked hard to build my confidence and believe in myself. Instead of dwelling on the past, I've learned to accept things as they are and move forward. I've stopped obsessing over social media and started dedicating my time to things that truly matter to me, like getting my driver's license, finishing my book, and pursuing further education. I'm proud to say that I'm a better version of myself now.

You've overcome the pain, and you'll overcome the process of healing too. At first, healing feels hard, especially when you're trying to break old habits. It's strange and different when someone you're used to having around suddenly isn't there anymore. You might have trouble sleeping, lose your appetite, cry at night, daydream about them, hope they'll change, feel a heavy weight on your chest, can't stop thinking about them, and even check their social media, which can make you anxious. But all these feelings are part of the healing process. The most important thing is that you don't want to stay stuck in this situation forever. You have to make a strong decision to change and move on. Holding onto hope can slow down your healing.

I have to admit, the first two weeks of my healing journey were extremely tough, but I knew it was all necessary for my growth. Each day, I got a little bit better because I knew I deserved better. I started to truly forgive and love myself. I began taking better care of myself, and most importantly, I started pursuing my goals and dreams. Instead of chasing after people or relationships, I believed in the idea that "if it's meant to be, it will happen." This way of thinking brought me clarity and peace of mind.

Stay consistent and maintain strong self-control. Understand your own worth and value, and never accept anything less than what you deserve. It's time to prioritize your aspirations and focus on your own growth and happiness rather than seeking validation through relationships.

Chapter 4
Healing Stages

Stage 1: Desperate for Answers – Random Thoughts #1

The intense desire to understand what went wrong can be exhausting. It fills your mind, leaving little room for anything else, and it can lead you to question your own worth, making you feel unworthy of love. You might find yourself desperately seeking answers about why your partner left. Without even realizing it, you could start behaving in ways that aren't healthy, like becoming paranoid, constantly checking up on them, or feeling sorry for yourself. It's a sad truth that our first heartbreak often changes us, sometimes triggering trauma.

While these feelings may not apply to everyone who has gone through a breakup, they come from my personal experiences, which some of you might relate to. Dealing with the initial stage of healing, where you crave answers, is tough. You might wonder if begging and chasing after your ex will make them treat you better or change their mind. But the reality is, it won't. Acting desperate only pushes them further away, lowering your own energy.

Before pouring your heart out to them, consider how they made you feel and whether they deserve such vulnerability from you. It's okay to feel hurt, but remember your self-respect and value. You don't need to seek closure from them because you already have it within yourself. You've done your best to make the relationship work, but you can't force someone to love you or stay with you. Genuine love shouldn't feel forced.

Ultimately, it's important to recognize your own worth and value. Believe that what's meant for you will come to you. Embrace this belief, let go of the need for a specific outcome, and focus on your own well-being. Sometimes, choosing peace means letting go, even if it hurts.

Stage 2: Denial and Anger – Random Thoughts #2

Denial is when you refuse to accept the truth, even when it's staring you in the face. You might find yourself thinking, "This can't be happening," "I can't imagine life without them," or "They love me, they just need space." These are all examples of denying reality when dealing with a breakup. You start doubting your own worth, believing that if you had done things differently, maybe they would still be with you.

But it's time to stop fooling yourself. Don't let yourself be manipulated or believe their excuses. Relationships are simple: if someone truly loves you, they'll stick around, no matter what challenges arise. Don't let them blame you or make you feel like it's all your fault. Face the truth, learn from it, and use it to become a better version of yourself.

Don't waste your time and energy trying to prove to them what they've lost. Instead, start the grieving process. It's okay to feel sad and blue; it's all part of healing. Remember, there's a rainbow after the rain. You're not alone in this.

Allow yourself to grieve. Cry if you need to; it's a natural part of the process and will ultimately make you feel better. Fight the urge to contact your ex, even though it's tempting. This is your chance to regain control over your emotions and begin the healing journey.

Make a list of all the negative aspects of your ex and remind yourself why you don't need to hold onto them or the pain they caused. Embrace your anger—it's part of the healing process too. Use it to empower yourself, to remind yourself that you deserve more from a relationship.

Practice self-talk. Stand in front of the mirror and repeat affirmations like, "I deserve better," "I love and value myself," and "What's meant for me will find me." Your anger may be directed at your ex, the situation, or even yourself, but it's meant to empower you and guide you towards a brighter future. Remember, you deserve happiness and fulfillment in your relationships. Don't settle for less than you deserve.

Stage 3: Bargaining – Random Thoughts #3

Here we are again, facing the tempting urge to call or message your ex. I understand how painful it is, and maybe you're thinking you can convince them to give the relationship another shot. You might even promise to be a better partner this time. But please, stop and consider your dignity. Your ex made the decision to leave, so why go through the effort of proving your worth? Why beg? It's important to realize that the more you chase after them, the more they'll pull away.

I'm not here to judge; I understand that you still love them. But there's a saying, 'Don't waste your time chasing butterflies, mend your own garden, and the butterflies will come.' Instead of putting all the burden of fixing the relationship on yourself, focus on self-improvement. Work on yourself, invest your energy into becoming the best version of you. Hit the gym, explore new talents, pamper yourself at the salon, upgrade your wardrobe. Concentrate on what you have rather than what you've lost. Find happiness in being single. Remember, you didn't lose your ex, you rediscovered yourself.

When you become a better version of yourself, successful and radiant, you'll naturally attract better people, and your ex may regret leaving you once they see how much you've grown. During this phase, instead of obsessing over your ex, focus on yourself. Consider initiating a "no-contact" rule. Cut off all communication, resist the urge to check their social media, or stalk them. It's only prolonging your pain. Ignorance can bring clarity. Let them go. Through no contact, they'll come to recognize your true value, reminisce about the good times they spent with you, and perhaps regret their decision to break up. Act as if they don't exist.

If they do come back, set your standards high. Don't settle for less than what you deserve. Remember, self-love and self-respect should always come first.

Stage 4: Relapse – Random Thoughts #4

This experience is what we call withdrawal syndrome. It's a time when your emotions can feel like a rollercoaster, and the pain can seem unbearable. I've been through it myself, so I understand how tough it can be. At this stage, the temptation to go back to what hurt you might be strong, but don't lose hope. You're almost through it, nearing the final stage of moving on. It's a test of your belief in yourself—that you're worthy, valued, deserving of love, and not just an option, but someone special.

Maintain your self-respect and dignity as you fight against relapse. Addiction can be powerful, like a drug that's hard to shake off, but breaking free is possible. Seek support from therapy or confide in someone trustworthy who understands. Reading self-help books and treating yourself kindly can also help. Be grateful for what you have and protect your mental well-being. Engaging in acts of kindness, like offering food and water to those in need, can bring a sense of joy and fulfillment. Even sharing your wisdom is a small gesture of kindness.

I've found that choosing kindness, especially during moments of struggle, brings me happiness. You might find the same. Keeping a journal of things you're thankful for can reinforce this positivity. Remember, true happiness comes from within, not from others. Finding peace of mind is key to happiness, and there are many paths to it.

If you've already moved past this stage, be proud to say, "It's time to let go," without hesitation. Reflect on the pain you've endured and ask yourself why you'd want to go back to it. You have the power to choose happiness over staying in a painful situation. Change your mindset, commit to it, and don't look back.

Stage 5: Acceptance – Random Thoughts # 5

This stage is all about surrender, reaching a point where you say, "It is what it is." You're gradually accepting that perhaps you and your ex-partner weren't meant to be together, and that's okay. You're realizing your own worth and uniqueness as an individual. You're embracing the 'power of now', no longer letting yourself dwell on the past or worry excessively about the future. This is the letting go stage, where you accept that things didn't work out with your ex. It's like saying, "What happens, happens." You're starting to believe you might be meant for someone else.

At this stage, you're finding relief and peace. You understand that constantly trying to make things work isn't good for you. You recognize your own value and believe that you deserve love and happiness. It's a moment of gratitude and a step forward in leveling up in life. For some people, reaching this stage of acceptance might be easier, especially if they've experienced multiple breakups before. They've learned the importance of living in the moment and being present. They've also likely worked through past traumas and developed emotional intelligence, which helps them attract healthier relationships. It's often said that you attract what you are—if you have low self-esteem or negative energy, you're more likely to attract similar personalities into your life.

Acceptance is like a soothing balm on a wound, gently easing the pain of past hurts and allowing the process of healing to begin. It's about acknowledging the reality of what has happened without judgment or resistance. During your journey of healing, acceptance plays a vital role in helping individuals come to terms with their experiences, whether they be loss, trauma, or disappointment. It doesn't mean liking or condoning what has occurred, but rather embracing the truth of it and finding peace within that truth. Through acceptance, people can release the burden of denial and self-blame, freeing themselves to move forward with greater clarity and strength.

Moreover, acceptance fosters a sense of resilience and empowerment. When we accept the things we cannot change, we redirect our energy towards what we can control, thereby reclaiming our agency in our own lives. It's about finding the courage to let go of what we cannot alter and embracing the possibilities of the present moment. In this way, acceptance becomes a catalyst for growth and transformation, paving the way for new beginnings and opportunities. It allows individuals to rewrite their narratives, viewing themselves not as victims of their circumstances, but as survivors capable of overcoming adversity. Ultimately, acceptance is not a destination but a continuous journey—a journey towards self-discovery, healing, and inner peace.

Stage 6: Overcoming Trauma from Previous Relationship – Random Thoughts # 6

Reaching this final stage of healing, especially if you've been through traumatic relationships, can be a pivotal moment. Many may have struggled with self-confidence, insecurities, and trust issues, believing that most partners are untrustworthy due to past experiences. It's crucial not to rush into another relationship until you're fully healed. Jumping into a new relationship too soon is like putting a bandage over a still painful wound—it might cover it temporarily, but it won't heal it. While rebound relationships might seem like a quick fix, true healing doesn't come from another person—it comes from within. Facing your traumas, forgiving yourself, and recognizing your own worthiness are essential steps. It's natural to feel insecure after being cheated on, but it's important to remember that the issue lies with the person who cheated, not with you.

Rebuilding self-confidence involves self-care, improving your physical appearance, and focusing on positive mindset shifts. Engaging in acts of kindness, changing your mindset, and avoiding negativity are also crucial. Disconnecting from social media, avoiding triggers like breakup videos or sad music, and investing in self-help books and journaling can greatly aid in healing. Take your time to find someone new. Rushing into a relationship out of loneliness or sadness often leads to repeating the same cycle of heartbreak. Being content and whole on your own is better than being with the wrong person. Once you've healed and found happiness within yourself, you'll naturally attract the right person into your life. Trust that what's meant for you will come at the right time.

To fully heal, allow yourself to feel all the emotions—grief, anger, sadness—before finding your way back to happiness. It's about turning the page to the next chapter focused on yourself. Sometimes, cutting off contact with someone who caused you pain is necessary for your healing journey. Blocking them, deleting memories, and prioritizing self-care can aid in finding peace and moving forward. For some, stepping away from social media and embracing solitude can be crucial for mental peace during the healing process.

This stage is all about YOU. It's crucial to fully heal from past relationships that caused pain and trauma. You might have low self-esteem, insecurities, or anxieties. That's okay! But don't jump into another relationship to fill the void. It won't heal you. Take time to heal on your own. Don't use someone else as a rebound.

Focus on self-care: improve your physical health, write in a journal, and keep talking to your therapist if needed. Be kind to yourself and surround yourself with positivity. Get rid of negativity and anything that reminds you of your ex. Read self-help books, meditate, or take a break from social media – whatever helps you heal.

Random Thoughts of Healing

Remember

Be Patient

Don't rush into a new relationship. Being single is better than being with the wrong person. Focus on your own happiness. When you're whole and healed, the right relationship will find you. Healing takes time. Feel your emotions – sadness, anger, grief – and eventually, you'll start to feel better again. Sometimes, going no-contact with your ex is necessary for healing. Block them and remove reminders. This is a time for self-discovery and growth. Focus on becoming the best version of yourself, and love will follow!

Take your time to heal; it's like a journey that doesn't happen all at once. It requires courage and patience. Some days you'll feel okay, but other days might be tough. However, you have to believe in the process. Keep going steadily; that's the secret to success. Focus on improving yourself. Try not to dwell on the past or worry too much about the future because what's important is the present moment. Accept the healing process, even though change can be scary. Remember, you're capable of change, especially if it's for your own good. Pray and have faith in God. He allows you to face challenges because He knows you can overcome them and emerge stronger.

Patience is like a gentle breeze that guides us through the twists and turns of our healing journey. When we're on the path to recovery, it's natural to feel eager for quick results, but healing takes time, much like a delicate flower blooming in the sunlight. It's about embracing the process, allowing ourselves to heal at our own pace without rushing or forcing it. Just as a seed needs nurturing and care before it can grow into a strong tree, our wounds need time and tenderness to mend. Patience reminds us to be kind to ourselves, to acknowledge our progress no matter how small, and to trust that each step forward, no matter how tiny, brings us closer to wholeness.

In our healing journey, patience acts as a steady companion, offering solace during moments of uncertainty and doubt. It's the quiet voice that whispers, "You're doing the best you can," when setbacks arise. Patience teaches us resilience, showing us that even in the face of adversity, there is strength in perseverance. Like a river carving its path through the rocks, healing requires patience to navigate the obstacles that stand in our way. It's about surrendering everything to God and the flow of life, understanding that healing isn't linear but rather a journey of peaks and valleys. With patience as our guide, we learn to embrace the journey with open arms, knowing that with each passing day, we grow stronger, wiser, and more resilient than before.

Some changes are painful but necessary.

Isolate: Disconnect to Connect

Take a hiatus and return reinvigorated. To truly connect with yourself, it's important to take breaks from social media and anything else that triggers painful memories or obstruct your healing process. By disengaging from these distractions, you create space to focus on your inner self. Dedicate time to introspection, delving into the root causes of your pain and identifying steps toward healing and personal growth. This period of self-examination enhances self-awareness and propels you forward with positivity.

Sometimes, in order to truly understand ourselves and heal, we need to disconnect from the constant noise of the world around us. It's like turning off the buzzing TV to hear the whispers of our own thoughts. When we step away from the distractions, whether it's social media, work stress, or even just the hectic pace of everyday life, we create space to connect with our true selves. It's in these quiet moments that we can listen to our own hearts, untangle the knots in our minds, and start to piece together the puzzle of who we really are. Disconnecting may entail confronting uncomfortable truths or confronting emotions we've long avoided, but within that discomfort lies the prospect of growth and healing.

As we disconnect from the external chaos, we begin to reconnect with the core of our being. It's like returning to home base after wandering through a maze of distractions. In this space of self-connection, we can rediscover our passions, dreams, and desires. We can reflect on our experiences, learn from our mistakes, and envision the path forward with clarity. It's a journey of self-discovery and self-acceptance, where we embrace all facets of ourselves—the light and the shadow, the joy and the pain. Through this process, we cultivate a deeper sense of compassion and understanding for ourselves, laying the foundation for true healing and transformation. Disconnecting to connect is not about escaping reality but about diving deeper into our own truth, finding solace in our own company, and ultimately, emerging stronger and more whole.

Know Your Value

Understanding your value in your healing journey is like having a compass guiding you through rough terrain. It means recognizing your worth, understanding that you deserve to be treated with kindness and respect. This journey isn't just about fixing wounds; it's about rediscovering the beauty and strength within yourself. When you know your value, you set boundaries that protect your well-being, saying "No" to things that harm you and "Yes" to things that nurture your soul. It's realizing that seeking help isn't a sign of weakness but a brave step toward growth. Knowing your value empowers you to surround yourself with people who uplift and support you, rather than those who bring you down. It's about choosing self-love over self-doubt, understanding that you are deserving of happiness and peace. In your healing journey, knowing your value also means acknowledging your progress and celebrating your victories, no matter how small they may seem. It's about forgiving yourself for past mistakes and embracing your imperfections as part of what makes you uniquely beautiful. When you know your value, you cultivate a sense of resilience that helps you bounce back from setbacks and challenges. You learn to trust yourself and your instincts, realizing that you have the strength and wisdom to navigate whatever life throws your way. Knowing your value is not just about reaching a destination; it's about embracing the journey with all its ups and downs, knowing that you are worthy of every moment of growth and transformation along the way. Knowing your value is not settling for less.

When you understand your value, you recognize that your worth isn't defined by your wounds or the scars you carry, but by the strength you find in overcoming them. Your value lies in the resilience you show in facing adversity, in the courage it takes to confront your pain, and in the grace you offer yourself in moments of vulnerability. It's acknowledging that healing isn't a linear path, but a messy, winding road full of twists and turns. And through it all, knowing your value means honoring your journey, embracing the highs and lows, and trusting that each step forward, no matter how small, is a testament to your worthiness of love, peace, and healing.

When you understand your value in the healing process, you empower yourself to set boundaries that protect your emotional well-being. It's recognizing that you deserve to be treated with kindness, compassion, and respect, both by others and by yourself. Your value serves as a foundation upon which you can build a support network of people who uplift and encourage you, and who remind you of your inherent worth when you forget.

Be Busy in a Productive Way

During your healing journey, it's important to stay focused on genuinely improving yourself, rather than using it as a distraction. Avoid pretending to be busy while secretly checking your phone for messages or scrolling through social media to see what your ex is up to. Such behavior can hinder your healing process and make it harder to move on. Instead, dedicate your time and energy to activities that truly help you grow and heal, such as spending time with supportive friends, pursuing hobbies you enjoy, or learning new skills. By focusing on yourself and your own well-being, you'll be better equipped to move forward in a positive direction.

During a healing journey, keeping yourself busy in a productive way is like giving your mind and body a healthy workout. It's about finding activities that uplift your spirits and help you grow stronger each day. One way to stay productive is by engaging in hobbies or interests that bring you joy and fulfillment. Whether it's painting, gardening, or playing music, these activities serve as therapeutic outlets for your emotions and creativity, providing a sense of purpose and accomplishment while boosting your self-esteem and confidence.

Another way to stay productive during a healing journey is by setting small, achievable goals for yourself. These goals could be as simple as going for a daily walk, reading a chapter of a book, or learning a new recipe. By breaking down larger tasks into smaller steps, you create momentum that builds progress. Celebrating each accomplishment, no matter how small, keeps you motivated and focused on moving forward. Moreover, staying connected with supportive friends and family members can provide encouragement and accountability on your journey. Whether it's through regular phone calls, video chats, or in-person visits, surrounding yourself with positive influences helps you stay on track and reminds you that you're not alone.

By keeping yourself productively engaged, you're not only occupying your time constructively but also nurturing your mind, body, and soul as you continue to heal and grow. Find your passion, engage in activities you excel at, explore new hobbies, and nourish your brain and body through exercise. Do things that truly make you happy, even in the smallest of ways. Self-growth means getting better at being yourself. It's like a plant reaching for the sun, but instead of leaves, you're growing skills, wisdom, and understanding. It happens when you learn new things, try new experiences, and reflect on what you've been through. Sometimes it's challenging, akin to climbing a mountain, but each step makes you stronger. You might learn to be kinder to yourself and others or discover talents you never knew you had. It's about becoming more confident, resilient, and at peace with who you are. Self-growth isn't a race or a competition; it's a journey, and every step forward, no matter how small, is a victory.

The Very Common - Self-Love

Self-love means refusing to accept breadcrumbs and never settling for less. It's believing that you deserve more than minimal efforts and having standards and boundaries to proctect your heart. It's also about confidently saying "No" when you don't want to do something and wholeheartedly saying "Yes" when it aligns with your desires and benefits you. If you're not someone's cup of tea, that's okay. Their opinion doesn't define your worth because you're focusing on what truly matters to you. When you genuinely love yourself, there's no need for chasing, forcing, or begging. Self-love isn't selfish; it's essential for growth and healing. It involves recognizing your own worth and learning to embrace the unique individual you are, scars and all.

Cherishing yourself, flaws and all, is where real growth begins. When you love yourself, you grant yourself permission to heal. It's like saying, 'I matter, and I deserve happiness." So, throughout the healing journey, remember to treat yourself with kindness, acknowledge every small step forward, and affirm your worthiness of love and care.

Self-love during the healing journey acts as a reliable compass guiding you in the right direction. It entails knowing your worth and treating yourself with the same tenderness you would offer to a cherished friend. Without self-love, it's easy to get lost in the storm of negativity and doubt. However, nurturing self-love cultivates resilience and inner strength. It's akin to constructing a fortress around your heart, shielding it from the arrows of self-criticism and doubt. Thus, as you navigate the twists and turns of healing, remember to nourish yourself with self-love. It's not selfish; it's necessary. By loving yourself, you're not only healing your wounds but also paving the way for a brighter, more compassionate future.

The Very Popular - Self-Care

Self-care activities are the small acts of kindness you do for yourself to soothe your soul and mend your heart. One self-care activity might be taking a long, hot bath, letting the warm water wash away the stresses of the day. Another could be going for a quiet walk in nature, feeling the sun on your face and the earth beneath your feet. Sometimes, self-care means saying "No" to things that drain your energy and "Yes" to things that fill you with joy, such as spending time with loved ones or curling up with a good book. It's about tuning to your body and mind, and giving yourself what you need to feel complete again.

Self-care also means tending to your physical health by visiting to the gym, going to the salon, or treating yourself to a relaxing body massage. Consuming nourishing foods that fuel your body and ensuring you get enough rest to recharge your batteries are crucial aspects of the healing process. It's like equipping your body with the tools it needs to rejuvenate from the inside out. And let's not overlook the power of creativity! Engaging in activities like painting, writing, dancing, or even shopping for new makeup sets can be incredibly therapeutic, enabling you to express yourself and release pent-up emotions.

Self- Affirmation

It's about reassuring yourself, saying, 'Hey, I'm here for you, and you're doing great." Healing can be challenging at times, like navigating through a storm, but self-affirmation acts as your umbrella, shielding you from the rain and keeping you warm. It's about acknowledging your strengths, resilience, and inherent worth, even when circumstances feel uncertain. It's about recognizing the beauty of your individuality.

There are numerous effective self-affirmations I've come across on various platforms, such as "I am valuable," "I am worthy," "I am the prize," "I am deserving of love and respect just as I am," "I trust in my ability to overcome challenges," "I am deserving of happiness and joy in my life," "I embrace my flaws and imperfections as part of what makes me unique," "I am capable of achieving my goals and dreams." "I choose to let go of what I cannot control and focus on what I can," "I am enough, exactly as I am in this moment," "I forgive myself for past mistakes and allow myself to move forward," "I am surrounded by love and support from those who care about me," "I believe in my strength and resilience to face whatever comes my way," and many more.

Act of Kindness

I discovered that engaging in small acts of kindness helped me feel better as I navigated through my healing journey. One thing that proved particularly beneficial was simply being present for someone and listening to them an empathetic ear. I recall a specific instance when I was on a bus en route to Dubai. I sat beside a woman who appeared visibly distressed. Initiating a conversation with a friendly "hi", we began chatting. She shared her life struggles and challenges with me, and I mostly listened, offering nods of understanding and empathy. I attempted to provide comfort and advice, offering gentle pats on her shoulder and reassurances that everything happens for a reason, and that trust in the process is crucial. She expressed immense gratitude for our conversation that day, stating that it had truly brightened her mood and she already felt a sense of improvement.

Inspired by this experience, I created an Instagram page where I share my thoughts on healing. My aim is to convey the message that pain and adversity are integral parts of the healing journey, and that brighter days lie ahead. Over time, people began to notice and appreciate my posts. Some even shared them and reached out to express their gratitude for the uplifting quotes I shared, noting how it had brought them solace after reading them.

There are countless ways to extend your kindness to others, and I've found it immensely beneficial on my personal journey of healing. Bringing joy to someone else brings joy to me as well; it feels like I'm spreading blessings to them. I'll always remember the wise words of one of my closest friends: "God uses people to bless people." Sometimes, the support or encouragement you seek doesn't come from where you expect it. It might come from a friend, a family member, or even from an unexpected source. It's remarkable how often the assistance or kindness you've been longing for is bestowed upon you through random acts of kindness from others.

Detachment

I've touched on this topic before, but detaching from certain things can serve as an important initial step toward progress and healing. Detachment entails letting go of someone, a situation, or our expectations regarding outcomes. Holding on too tightly can impede our ability to move forward. It's crucial to reflect on why we're so attached. Perhaps it stems from past wounds. If that's the case, we need to practice self-forgiveness, self-care, and self-love. Once we've addressed the root causes of our attachment and worked on ourselves, we can begin to release our grip. The encouraging news is that detachment may not always yield negative consequences. In fact, it may lead to a realization of your worth when you're absent, prompting others to desire your return, or it may help you recognize your own value and choose not to seek their return. In either scenario, you emerge victorious.

No-Contact Rule

The "no-contact" rule acts as a protective shield you erect around yourself following a breakup. It involves cutting off all communication and contact with the person who caused you pain. While it may seem daunting, it's akin to granting yourself space to breathe and heal. Remaining in constant contact with someone who has hurt you is akin to reopening a wound repeatedly. Stepping away allows you the necessary time and distance to heal properly.

One of the biggest benefits of the "no-contact" rule is that it aids in reclaiming your sense of self. In relationships, particularly unhealthy ones, it's easy to lose sight of your identity as you become overly focused on the other person. By severing contact, you afford yourself the opportunity to rediscover who you are and discern what you truly want and need. It's akin to hitting the reset button on your life. Additionally, it enables you to process your emotions without external interference. Continuously engaging with the individual who caused you pain can hinder your ability to sort through your feelings. However, solitude allows you the space to reflect on what occurred and how it impacted you emotionally. While this process may be challenging, it's an integral aspect of the healing journey.

Overall, the "no-contact" rule offers you a fresh start and the chance to move forward in a healthier manner.

Know the Difference: Love vs. Attachment

At times, distinguishing between genuine love and mere attachment can be challenging. Signs of attachment often manifest as statements like "I can't live without you," or "You're my everything," accompanied by the belief that the individual is the sole source of your happiness or sorrow. Conversely, love entails both parties enriching each other's lives. Emotions aren't solely reliant on the other person, and both individuals prioritize personal growth while providing mutual support. While you derive joy from their presence, you also recognize that you would be okay even in their absence.

Chapter 5:
Random Thoughts of Healing - Inspirational and Motivational Quotes

During my journey of self-improvement, I've compiled quotes from my own reflections. I'm delighted to share these inspiring and motivating statements with you. You can utilize them to uplift your spirits and stay focused on positivity every day, or share them with your friends, family, and loved ones.

Random Thoughts of Healing Quote #1:

"Healing commences by recognizing when it's time to pause. Cease the illusions, halt the pursuit, refrain from chasing or pleading, and relinquish self-pity. It's time to rise and stride towards the next chapter of your journey."

Random Thoughts of Healing Quote #2:

"Heart asks: How do you know if you've moved on? Brain replies: When their presence or absence no longer affects you."

Random Thoughts of Healing Quote #3:

"Rejection is divine redirection. If someone rejects or overlooks you, it's the universe's way of guiding you towards the right path. Instead of doubting your worth, focus on self-improvement and becoming the best version of yourself."

Random Thoughts of Healing Quote #4:

"Success doesn't stem from sporadic actions; it arises from consistent effort."

Random Thoughts of Healing Quote #5:

"If you feel you don't belong and you have to chase or force someone or something, do not be afraid to let go. The right person and the right relationship will come to you naturally if you choose to let go of the wrong ones."

Random Thoughts of Healing Quote #6:

"Sometimes, stepping back helps you see your worth."

Random Thoughts of Healing Quote #7:

"It's okay to disconnect for a while; solitude fosters self-love and determination. Dream big! Return like a blossoming flower, captivating attention and admiration naturally."

Random Thoughts of Healing Quote #8:

"Know your worth! Choose peace over pieces. Refuse to settle for mere breadcrumbs when you deserve a feast."

Random Thoughts of Healing Quote #9:

"Find the silver lining in every day, even during the toughest moments."

Random Thoughts of Healing Quote #10:

"Embrace your current journey, even if it diverges from your expectations. Every season serves a purpose until you are ready to claim what's rightfully yours".

Random Thoughts of Healing Quote #11:

"Utilize your pain to reconstruct your life instead of succumbing to despair. Pain signals that it's time to shine. Remember, even the moon brightens the darkest nights."

Random Thoughts of Healing Quote #12:

"Feel all the feels! It's okay not to be okay! Be sad, be mad, be lonely, be messy, and be crazy. Those emotions are valid and part of your healing journey. Trust the process and everything will be alright."

Random Thoughts of Healing Quote #13:

"If I'm not your cup of tea, I won't be mad, sad or pity, I'd rather focus on feeling blessed, grateful, and excited for what's to come. We can't please everyone, and that's alright."

Random Thoughts of Healing Quote #14:

"Always choose yourself and learn to detach from a person or situation. Detachment may have two possible outcomes, they may realize your worth when you're gone and come back, or you'll realize your worth and not want them to come back. Either way, you win".

Random Thoughts of Healing Quote #15:

"Letting go of the things I can't control brings calmness while working on things that I can control brings peace."

Random Thoughts of Healing Quote #16:

"Stop chasing butterflies rather mend your own garden so butterflies will come."

Random Thoughts of Healing Quote #17:

"Don't worry about those who shuts doors on you. Trust in God's plan. New doors will open when you let go and keep moving forward. Have faith and keep going!"

Random Thoughts of Healing Quote #18:

"Healthy relationships require space. Have a moment to miss each other, grow individually yet always support one another."

Random Thoughts of Healing Quote #19:

"Some people, regardless of what they lack—money, looks, or social connections—always radiate with energy and confidence."

Random Thoughts of Healing Quote #20:

"Sometimes, falling apart leads you exactly where you need to be."

Random Thoughts of Healing Quote #21:

"Even when things seem tough, believe that better times are ahead. It's normal to stumble along the way, but what's important is to keep trying to improve."

Random Thoughts of Healing Quote #22:

"Having a dream without taking action is like imagining things that aren't real. It's important to not only dream big but also to work hard to make those dreams come true. Take steps every day towards your goals, no matter how small they may seem. Stay focused and persistent, and you'll turn your visions into reality!"

Random Thoughts of Healing Quote #23:

"We are only given a chance to live once, so let's enjoy life and just be happy. No hate, no bitterness, no self-pity and just simply be happy."

Random Thoughts of Healing Quote #24:

"Your story may not have to have such a happy beginning but it doesn't make who you are. It is the rest of your story—who you choose to be that matters." - from Kung Fu Panda movie.

Random Thoughts of Healing Quote #25:

"Don't give up! The hardest battles are given to the strongest soldiers!"

Random Thoughts of Healing Quote #26:

"Healing starts with awareness, recognizing how this style has influenced your life. It's about making peace with the past, forgiving those who left, and learning to trust again, both in yourself and in others."

Random Thoughts of Healing Quote #27:

"But remember, it's never too late to change our habits, our outlook, and ultimately, ourselves. Let go of relationships that only offer the bare minimum, and recognize that clinging to someone who doesn't value you is a sign of lacking self-respect."

Random Thoughts of Healing Quote #28:

"Healing can be challenging. There are ups and downs, good days and bad days, but I believe it's all part of the journey."

Random Thoughts of Healing Quote #29:

"Knowing your value empowers you to surround yourself with people who uplift and support you, rather than those who bring you down. It's about choosing self-love over self-doubt, understanding that you are deserving of happiness and peace."

Random Thoughts of Healing Quote #30:

"God uses people to bless people. Sometimes, the support or encouragement you seek doesn't come from where you expect it. It might come from a friend, a family member, or even from an unexpected source."

Random Thoughts of Healing Quote #31:

"Not all storms come to disrupt your life; some come to clear your path."

Random Thoughts of Healing Quote #32:

"Constructive criticism is better than fake compliments. Embrace the challenges; they lead to growth and improvement."

Random Thoughts of Healing Quote #33:

"Feeling hurt, angry, or disrespected? Leave silently and never look back. Silence and absence are great revenge."

Random Thoughts of Healing Quote #34:

"Just you being you is all you need when you're with the right person. If you ever doubt your worth, it's time to hit the road, babe! You deserve the best, so don't settle for anything less."

Random Thoughts of Healing Quote #35:

"You're already complete just as you are. No need to please anyone. Stop comparing yourself to others because the only race worth running is against who you were yesterday. Focus on becoming the best version of yourself!"

Random Thoughts of Healing Quote #36:

"Find your place where you're cherished and valued. Don't waste time in the wrong crowd and feel hurt when your worth isn't recognized. Surround yourself with those who truly appreciate you. Don't settle where your value goes unnoticed. "

Random Thoughts of Healing Quote #37:

"Glow up from within! Invest in yourself, embrace your unique beauty, and ditch the need to fit in. Be YOU!"

Random Thoughts of Healing Quote #38:

"Trust your instincts! If it doesn't feel right, it's okay to walk away. Don't force anything that doesn't resonate with you."

Random Thoughts of Healing Quote #39:

"Respect yourself enough to refuse anything less than you deserve. You're worthy of more than just scraps and the bare minimum. You deserve to be chosen and to be treated the way you want to be treated."

Random Thoughts of Healing Quote #40:

"Someday, you'll look back and say, 'Wow, I made it!' Keep pushing forward because that day is coming."

Random Thoughts of Healing Quote #41:

"You have to go through tough times to get to the good stuff."

Random Thoughts of Healing Quote #42:

"The way others treat me comes from how I treat myself. It's all about what's inside me. If I want others to treat me well, I have to treat myself well first."

Random Thoughts of Healing Quote #43:

"When it's real love, there's no need for chasing or forcing things. Love should feel easy, not heavy."

Random Thoughts of Healing Quote #44:

"Let go of relationships that only offer bare minimum, and recognize that clinging to someone who doesn't value you is a sign of lacking self-respect."

Random Thoughts of Healing Quote #45:

"I've learned to let go of overthinking and find peace within myself. No longer do I seek validation from others; if my presence isn't appreciated, I gracefully step aside."

Random Thoughts of Healing Quote #46:

"Life's complexities are often of our own making, so I've embraced simplicity."

Random Thoughts of Healing Quote #47:

"Every goodbye brings a fresh start."

Random Thoughts of Healing Quote #48:

"Embrace both praise and feedback. Like a flower, growth requires both sunshine and rain."

Random Thoughts of Healing Quote #49:

"Don't compare yourself with the achievements of others. Your only competition is who you were yesterday. We all have our own passions to explore, which is why the sizes of our fingers are not the same. We are each unique in our own way."

Random Thoughts of Healing Quote #50:

"Don't stop working on yourself and aspiring to achieve your goals. Act now before it's too late. Use the pain to rebrand your life and come back stronger."

Random Thoughts of Healing Quote #51:

"Accept both compliments and criticism, because a flower must have both raindrops and sunlight to grow."

Random Thoughts of Healing Quote #52:

"Instead of dwelling on the past, we should be grateful for the lessons we've learned from pain and suffering. Those tough times made us stronger and wiser."

Random Thoughts of Healing Quote #53:

"Breaking up might feel like a failure to some, but to others, it's a valuable lesson learned. Think of it as a chapter in a book where we gain insight and wisdom."

Random Thoughts of Healing Quote #54:

"Regret is like a big, bad enemy, but taking risks isn't scary. So go ahead, take those risks instead of looking back with regret. Sure, you might trip and fall along the way, but that's where you find your strength and bravery."

Random Thoughts of Healing Quote #55:

"We can't undo what's already happened, but we hold the key to our future by letting go of past hurts."

Random Thoughts of Healing Quote #56:

"Even when the times are hard, believe that better days are coming your way."

Random Thoughts of Healing Quote #57:

"Life has taught me that not everyone is up for change. Some people just want to stay the same forever. Change might be scary, but it's the only way to grow."

Random Thoughts of Healing Quote #58:

"Don't see yourself as a victim; focus on the positive. Stop believing that you're not worthy just because someone left you. You are enough, and the right person will see that, even if you haven't done anything extraordinary to win them over."

Random Thoughts of Healing Quote #59:

"Relying on others for your emotional needs leaves you vulnerable when they're not available. Instead, build your own emotional support system to rely on yourself."

Random Thoughts of Healing Quote #60:

"You made it through the hurt; you will make it through the healing."

Random Thoughts of Healing Quote #61:

"Patience teaches us resilience, showing us that even in the face of adversity, there is strength in perseverance."

Random Thoughts of Healing Quote #62:

"Knowing your value means honoring your journey, embracing the highs and lows, and trusting that each step forward, no matter how small, is a testament to your worthiness of love, peace, and healing."

Random Thoughts of Healing Quote #63:

"You need to cherish yourself, flaws and all, because that's where real growth begins."

Random Thoughts of Healing Quote #64:

"I will keep chasing nonstop, but this time, I will chase my dreams and goals, not people and relationships"

Random Thoughts of Healing Quote #65:

"Change is scary but necessary for your growth."

Random Thoughts of Healing - Letting Go

It's time to bid farewell,

No longer swayed by your rationale.

It's time to say goodbye,

Your words won't twist my mind anymore.

It's time to part ways,

Your constant presence brings pain.

It's time to release,

Ending the futile dreams of reunion.

It's time to break free,

Your casual involvement wounds.

It's time to reclaim,

Before dignity and self-respect fade.

Random Thoughts of Healing

It's time to move forward,

Embracing healing and renewal.

It's time to let go,

To find joy beyond the memory of you.

Random Thoughts of Healing - You are Valuable

Who among you has experienced the feeling of not being valued by someone? How about not being chosen by someone? How does it feel? Painful, right? Have you felt unworthy about yourself? Do you even know your value and self-worth? If not, then let me tell you a story that might enlighten you and help you decide to give up and move on if you are trapped in that situation.

There was a short story about a father who gave an old watch to his son before he died. A father said to his son, "Here is a watch that your grandfather gave me, and it is almost 200 years old. Before I give it to you, go to the jewelry store downtown, tell them that I want to sell it and see how much they offer you."

The son went to the jewelry store, came back to his father and said, "They offered $150.00 only because it is so old."

The father said, "Go to the pawnshop" .

The son went to the pawnshop, came back to his father and said, "The pawnshop offered $10.00 only because it looks so worn."

The father asked his son to go to the museum and show them the watch.

He went to the museum, came back and said to his father, "The curator offered $500,000.00 for this rare piece to be included in the precious antique collections!"

The father said, "See, I wanted to let you know that the right place values you in the right way. Don't find yourself in the wrong place and get angry if you are not being valued. Those that know your value are those who appreciate you. Don't stay in a place where nobody sees your value."

It is truly an inspiring story, especially for those people who felt unworthy, unappreciated and undervalued just because they are in the wrong place, wrong relationships, and with the ewrong people. If you feel you don't belong and you have to chase or force something or someone, do not be afraid to let go. The right job, right people, and right relationships will come to you naturally if you choose to let go of the wrong ones. Protect your peace and well-being. Invest in your growth, be your beautiful self, and you do not need to fit into someone else's box. Nourish your brain, study, read novels, read self-help books. and learn new things. Glow up! Go to the gym and pamper yourself! Say "No" when you want to and if it turns off people, so be it! Say "Yes" when you want to; you don't need to seek permission to do what feels right for you. Follow your gut! If it doesn't feel right, walk away, and do not force things.

Random Thoughts of Healing

Set standards and boundaries because setting boundaries and standard for yourself is like creating a personal rule book that guides how you want to be treated and how will interact with people. It is about defining your limits and expectations to ensure you maintain your well-being and honor your values. Think of it as drawing a clear line between what is acceptable and what is not, empowering you to live authentically and respect your own needs.

Heal! When people say that healing is more painful than the wound, I agree! The journey of healing is not constant; rather, it is changes over time. Some days you feel okay, fine, and happy, and some days you feel sad and lonely, and both days are okay and valid. Learn to respect yourself by not accepting the bare minimum and breadcrumbs because you deserve better. You deserve to be chosen and to be treated the way you want to be treated. Heal gently and allow yourself to cry. The healing journey must consist of bumpy roads and roller coaster rides; hence, allow yourself to feel those types of emotions. Let it flow and feel the pain because someday you will get there until it doesn't hurt anymore. Then you will finally breathe the air of peace and relief. When the time is right, when the intention is pure and your heart is ready, God will surely let you experience being loved by the person meant for you.

You yourself are already enough and you don't need to be a people pleaser, and you don't need to compare yourself to others as the only competition you have is who you were yesterday and how to become a better version of yourself.

Remember that you are valuable, you are a unique individual, you are authentic, and you are beautiful!

Random Thoughts of Healing - Aspire to Achieve

Have you ever dreamed of something big or manifesting something you want? Maybe you wanted to be an actress entertaining people, a writer sharing wisdom and knowledge with people, or the CEO of your own company. Those dreams, those wishes for something more, that's what "aspiring to achieve" is all about. It's about having a goal, something you set your sights on and work towards making real. Think of it like climbing a mountain. At the bottom, you see this giant peak reaching towards the clouds. It seems impossible, too high to ever reach. But then you take that first step, and another, and another. Maybe it's hard, maybe there are rocks in the way, but you keep going because you know the amazing view that awaits you at the top.

Eleven years ago, I was having a tough time with money, and I really wanted to work in another country to earn more and support my family better. My passport was almost expired at that time. I went outside the house, looked at the stars, and said to myself, "I won't let my passport expire without finding a job abroad." And now, here I am, working at a great company in the United Arab Emirates, earning enough to take care of my family's needs. I turned my dream into reality.

That's what aspiring to achieve feels like. You might have a big dream, your mountain to climb, but you don't need to reach the top all at once. You just need to start taking steps, even small ones, in the right direction. You need to imagine yourself, feel the happiness and act as if your dreams are real, and it will be guaranteed to happen as long as you follow some tips I have collected and gathered in aspiring to achieve my dreams.

1. Know your passion: The first step is figuring out what makes your heart race. What are you good at? What things do you enjoy doing so much that you lose track of time? Maybe you love acting, writing stories, or drawing pictures. That spark, that thing that excites you, can be the starting point for your dreams. In my case, I love writing, and I am aspiring myself to have my own in the near future.

2. Make a list of your achievable goals: Once you have your spark, break down your big dream into smaller, achievable goals. Remember the mountain? You wouldn't try to climb it in one giant leap, would you? Instead, you'd set milestones – reaching a certain point by lunchtime, taking a break at a specific rock. In my case, I am writing at least 500 words per day to achieve 40,000 words as one of the requirements for publishing a self-help book.

3. Draft, Scratch and Start: Now that you have your goals, figure out how to get there. In my case, my target is 90 days, and I am making sure that I am consistent with my writings on a daily basis. Enjoy what are you doing because there are points in your life that you will get lazy and bored, but never give up.

4. Keep Going! The road to achieving your dreams isn't always easy. There will be times you get discouraged, times you want to quit. But remember, even the most experienced

climbers have to rest sometimes. Don't let setbacks stop you. Learn from them, adjust your plan if needed, and keep climbing and keep going.

5. Celebrate Milestone: Reaching the top of your mountain is an overwhelming feeling, but don't forget to celebrate all the smaller victories along the way. Recognizing your progress keeps you motivated and reminds you of how far you've come.

Aspiring to achieve isn't just about reaching the top. It's about the journey, the learning, and the amazing person you become along the way. You may hear discouragement from people around you; ignore them and listen to your gut. So, keep reaching for the stars, one step at a time. Remember, even the biggest dreams start with a single wish and the courage to take that first step. Now go out there and chase yours! Remember, there is no gain without pain. Rewards require dedication and determination.

Certainly! An expanded version with more details, tips, and tricks for this topic is written in my next book entitled "Bucket List - Aspire to Achieve".

www.ingramcontent.com/pod-product-compliance
Lightning Source LLC
Chambersburg PA
CBHW072101110526
44590CB00018B/3260